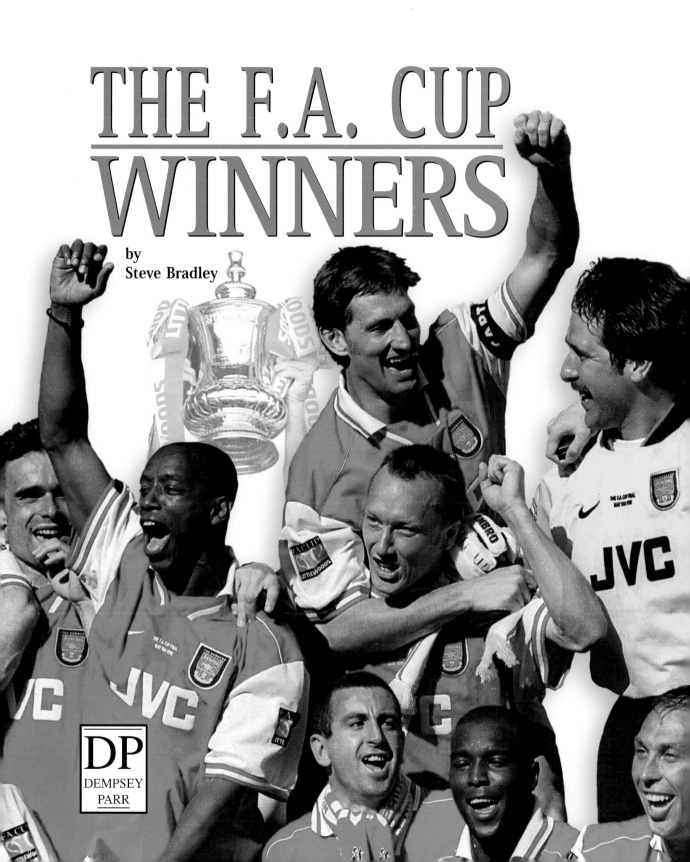

THE F.A. CUP
WINNERS

by
Steve Bradley

DP

DEMPSEY
PARR

THE F.A. CUP
WINNERS

First published in Great Britain in 1998 by
Dempsey Parr
13 Whiteladies Road
Clifton
Bristol BS8 1PB

ISBN: 1-84084-206-7

Produced for Dempsey Parr by Prima Creative Services

Editorial director Roger Kean
Managing editor Steve Faragher (Content E.D.B.)
Designer Maryanne Booth (Content E.D.B.)
Repro by Prima Creative Services

Printed and bound in Italy

Acknowledgements
The publisher would like to thank Tim Smith (Content E.D.B) , Mark Taylor and Richard Jones for their invaluable help in the production of this book.

Picture Acknowledgements
The publisher would like to thank Allsport for their help and the kind permission to reproduce the photographs used in this book.

One year ago: Gianluca Vialli and Gianfranco Zola lift the FA Cup in celebration after defeating Middlesbrough 2-0 on 17th May 1997.

Introduction

Dreaming of the Twin Towers...

Every year, millions of people around the world tune in to watch a football match played in a North London suburb. The FA Cup has, and always will be, the best cup competition of them all...

It's corny, but true. The FA Cup is a great leveller. In what other competition could little Emley compete on even terms with West Ham United? Were they to play the Hammers at Upton Park in a league game, they would probably ship five or six goals. But add the magical ingredient of the FA Cup, and suddenly Emley's collection of postmen, fitters and salesmen can battle with the best in the land. It's the one chance that non-league players get to pit their wits against the best.

For Stevenage, this season's cup was their day in *The Sun*. They almost switched their cup tie against Newcastle to St James' Park to cash-in on a guaranteed full-house. But the tabloid newspaper stepped in and sponsored the tie which became the most talked-about match of the season.

Every year, the drama of the cup unfolds, bringing with it great tales of incident, upset and heroism. Here is the story of this season's FA Cup, the most famous domestic competition in the world...

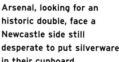

Dennis Wise lifts the FA Cup last year after Chelsea beat Middlesbrough 2-0

Qualifying Rounds

The FA Cup is without doubt the most historic and romantic domestic cup competition in the world. The first final was in 1872, when Wanderers defeated the Royal Engineers 1-0 at the Kennington Oval and it's been played ever since, interrupted only by the two World Wars. Manchester United have lifted the famous trophy a record nine times, but the great romance surrounding the competition is the fact that non-league teams can enter, in the hope of qualifying to meet the giants of the modern game.

The FA Cup is split into two parts; a qualifying phase, followed by the competition proper. The non-league teams, barring certain exemptions, must qualify through four rounds before the First Round proper when the clubs from the Second and Third Divisions enter.

PRELIMINARY ROUND	This is played if more than 304 teams enter the competition (not including the best 24 non-league sides and 92 league clubs).
QUALIFYING ROUNDS (304 TEAMS)	There are four qualifying rounds. In the First Qualifying Round 304 teams play in 36 regional divisions, each containing eight teams. These ties are pre-determined from the off, so there is no draw for the Second and Third Qualifying Rounds.
FOURTH QUALIFYING ROUND (56 TEAMS)	The 36 group winners join 20 exempt non-league teams (those with the best cup pedigree in recent seasons) for the Fourth Qualifying Round. The 20 teams exempt for this season's FA Cup were... Altrincham, Ashford Town, Boreham Wood, Boston United, Colwyn Bay, Enfield, Farnborough Town, Hayes, Hendon, Hereford United, Kidderminster Harriers, Morecambe, Northwich Victoria, Runcorn, Rushden & Diamonds, Southport, St Albans, Stalybridge Celtic, Sudbury Town, Wisbech Town.
FIRST ROUND PROPER (80 TEAMS)	The 28 qualifiers join the 48 Nationwide Division Two and Three teams for the First Round, which is drawn on a regional basis between north and south. They're joined by four more non-league exemptions: the two teams from the previous season's FA Trophy final (Dagenham & Redbridge and Woking), plus two sides the Football Association deems to have the best recent pedigree - in this case, Stevenage Borough and Hednesford Town.
SECOND ROUND (40 TEAMS)	The 80 teams from the First Round are halved to 40 for the second, but again, the draw is on a regional basis, split between north and south.
THIRD ROUND (64 TEAMS)	The big one! All the teams from the Premiership and Nationwide Division One join in for the Third Round which is always played in early January. The draw is completely open and for many fans, this is the most exciting day of the season.

Wembley Stadium: The home of English football and the venue for the FA Cup Final

FA Cup Round One
Here come the professionals...

Mark Hateley, the former England and AC Milan striker suffered the indignation of seeing his Hull team knocked out of the cup by Hednesford Town. And it wasn't the only upset of the round...

The 48 teams from Divisions Two and Three of Nationwide League joined the FA Cup in the first round and not all of them survived to tell the tale. Basingstoke of the Ryman Premier League held Wycombe Wanderers at Adams Park, before dispatching the Division Two side in the replay. Coombs' 85th minute spot-kick for Basingstoke took the tie into extra-time and they held their collective nerve to win the penalty shoot-out 5-4.

Six months after Brighton's victory at Edgar Street condemned Hereford to life outside the Nationwide League, Graham Turner's men gained sweet revenge by sending the Seagulls crashing out of the FA Cup. Brighton boss Steve Gritt had no complaints about the result. "Hereford worked very hard and obviously felt they had something to prove after our result here last season."

Former England and AC Milan hitman Mark Hateley has found life in the lower echelons of the Nationwide League difficult to come to terms with. With his charges, Hull City, struggling at the wrong end of the Third Division, the man who once lived in the lap of luxury in Monaco suffered the indignation of seeing his team dumped out of the FA Cup by non-league Hednesford. A deflated Hateley said: "Hednesford showed there is very little difference between the Conference and the Third Division." And in another First Round shock, Hendon beat London rivals Leyton Orient. Although they were held in the first game on their own turf, Hendon overcame Orient 1-0 at Brisbane Road.

Last season's beaten semi-finalists Chesterfield were booed off by their own fans after struggling to overcome GM Vauxhall Conference side Northwich Victoria. The Spireites' goal came in the fifth minute from former Carlisle United striker David Reeves.

Fulham bosses Kevin Keegan and Ray Wilkins suffered an early shock at their high profile clash with Margate,

> **"We can now pay the players for the next three weeks."**
> Hereford boss Graham Turner, after they made £28,000 profit in the tie against Brighton.

> **"When we took over the club, we said it would take three years to turn around. And we're still sticking by that."**
> Hull City owner and tennis club supremo David Lloyd, after the East Yorkshiremen were dumped out of the cup by Hednesford Town.

> **"It's a bit different from 13 years ago."**
> Gainsborough Trinity keeper Steve Sherwood, who played in Watford's FA Cup final defeat against Everton in 1984.

AT A GLANCE...

Non-league teams who triumphed in the first round over league opposition.

Basingstoke	(Wycombe)
Hendon	(Leyton Orient)
Hereford	(Brighton)
Hednesford	(Hull)

WHO PLAYS IN THE FIRST ROUND...

The First Round proper is when the 48 teams from Nationwide League Divisions Two and Three join the competition. Also in the hat are the 28 teams who progressed from the qualifying round and four exempt semi-professional sides to give a grand total of 80. Two of the exempted four are the teams that contested the previous season's FA Trophy Final, plus the two non-league sides the FA deems the best from the last campaign. The four this season were Dagenham & Redbridge, Hednesford Town, Stevenage Borough and Woking. The First Round draw is split between north and south.

Buster Bloodvessel, Margate's chairman, displays his goal celebration technique

The story of Round One...

when the team sponsored by pop group Bad Manners took the lead after only six minutes. The Londoners drew level in the 23rd minute and Rob Scott scored Fulham's winner, converting Paul Peschisolido's low cross six minutes from time. "Margate were well organised and we're just pleased to be in the hat for the second round," said a relieved Keegan.

Two high profile goalkeepers of yesteryear saw their non-league sides defeated by league opposition. John Burridge, in his 29th season in the game conceded four goals as Blyth Spartans tumbled at Blackpool. Gainsborough Trinity's Steve Sherwood, who

> "We gave a good account of ourselves and we're going home with our pride intact."
>
> Colwyn Bay boss Bryn Jones after his team were beaten 2-0 by Third Division champions Notts County.

played in the 1984 FA Cup final for Watford against Everton saw his side defeated by Lincoln City. Notts County overcame Unibond Premier League side Colwyn Bay. Graeme Hogg's goal settled the issue.

Former Liverpool striker Ronnie Rosenthal scored twice for Graham Taylor's high-flying Watford against Barnet.

FA Cup Round Two
Little Emley march on...

Emley, Stevenage Borough and former Nationwide League side Hereford United all overcame league opposition. And Walsall destroyed Macclesfield 7-0, their only home defeat of the season...

Only three non-league teams overcame league opposition in the second round of the FA Cup. Unibond League Premier side Emley emerged victorious after a mammoth battle against Lincoln City. The

West Yorkshire minnows thought they had won the initial tie at Sincil Bank only for the Imps' Tony Fleming to snatch an equaliser eight minutes into time added on. "The referee seemed to find

> "We had the drainage done last year and there are still about 100 drainage channels showing. You run along and you fall down the things."
>
> Basingstoke boss Ernie Howe on the pitch problems at their Camrose ground.

time from nowhere," commented Emley striker Glynn Hurst afterwards. However, it was Emley who scored a late goal to send the replay into extra time, before they struck the decisive spot kick in the resultant penalty shoot-out.

Stevenage Borough earned a Third Round draw at First Division Swindon with a hard fought victory against Cambridge United. The GM

WHO PLAYS IN THE SECOND ROUND...

The 80 teams from the First Round are whittled down to 40. Like the First Round, the draw is loosely split on a regional basis between north and south. Winners here get the opportunity to take on the giants.

Guiliano Grazioli of Stevenage Borough was one of the heroes of this year's Cup

The story of Round Two...

Vauxhall Conference side were just seven minutes away from beating Cambridge at the first hurdle. Gary Crawshaw's penalty in the 17th minute gave Borough the lead but United equalised late in the game. Stevenage, backed by a crowd of 4,886 at Broadhall Way won the replay 2-1.

Hereford striker Neil Grayson continued his excellent scoring form with a goal in each of the Bulls' hard fought ties against Colchester. The 33-year-old Conference striker, who, in the previous round had scored a brace against Brighton, struck the equaliser at Layer Road to earn the Bulls a replay and then repeated the trick to send this Second Round tie into extra time. Hereford manager Graham Turner sang Grayson's praises after the 5-4 penalty shoot-out victory. "He's a handful for any defence and always gets two or three chances," said the Bulls' boss. "And there's not much chance of him passing when he gets near goal."

Veteran Peterborough striker Jimmy Quinn struck twice to send Conference side Dagenham & Redbridge crashing out of the FA Cup. The ex-Reading boss, 38, scored

two priceless late goals after Dagenham had lead Barry Fry's Posh 2-1, but it left Quinn in a dilemma whether to take up an offer from Bournemouth as player-coach. "None of lads want me to leave," said the Irishman, who once took Reading to within sight of the Premiership in the play-offs. Quinn stayed at Peterborough, only to see them defeated at home in the next round to Walsall. Walsall's 7-0 victory away at Macclesfield was perhaps the best performance of the round, coming, as it did, at the ground which held the longest unbeaten home league record of all 92 clubs in 1997/98. Macclesfield were later promoted, their league record still intact.

Fulham progressed with a 1-0 win over Southend, but boss Ray Wilkins wasn't best pleased with his team. "That's our worst performance since I came here," he blasted. Wilkins was sacked just days before Fulham met Grimsby in the Second Division play-offs. The decision was said to have been made by Kevin Keegan, who took the management reins.

Trouble flared at Scunthorpe when police were forced to fire CS gas at visiting

Ilkeston Town fans. The game finished all-square but Scunthorpe won the replay 2-1.

A capacity crowd at Hednesford, conquerors of Hull City in the previous round, saw Darlington triumph over the Conference side. Darren Roberts' 70th minute penalty settled the match. Last season's semi-finalists Chesterfield fell at the second hurdle this time around. Although John Duncan's charges managed a draw at Blundell Park, Grimsby won the replay 2-0.

Basingstoke took Northampton all the way, but the non-league side were narrowly defeated 5-4 in a penalty shoot-out in the replay. Kings Lynn didn't fare quite so well in their tie against Rotherham. The Dr Martens League team were beaten 6-0 at Milmoor. Third Division pace-setters Notts County fell to Preston North End. David Eyres struck Preston's winner in the 96th minute after the tie had gone to a replay.

In the round's only all non-league match, Cheltenham overcame Boreham Wood to earn a tie at First Division Reading. The Gloucestershire side won 2-0 in the replay.

Mark Hateley's Hull City were dumped out of the Cup by non-league Hednesford Town

Paul Peschisolido: Fulham's striker in full flow against Southend United

Round Two quiz

Test your football knowledge

1 Which team did veteran keeper John Burridge play for in this season's cup?
a) Emley   b) Blyth Spartans   c) Gainsborough Trinity

2 In which year did Burnley win their only FA Cup trophy?
a) 1910   b) 1912   c) 1914

3 Who became the only non-English club to lift the trophy in 1927 when they beat Arsenal 2-1?
a) Newport County   b) Swansea City   c) Cardiff City

4 Where do Colchester United play?
a) Griffin Park   b) Layer Road   c) Adams Park

5 In which county is non-league Emley situated?
a) West Yorkshire   b) Lincolnshire   c) Nottinghamshire

6 What nationality is Walsall's Roger Boli?
a) French   b) Ghanaian   c) South African

7 Which famous ex-Chelsea player appeared for Cheltenham Town in this season's cup?
a) John Bumstead   b) Clive Walker   c) Kerry Dixon

8 Bristol Rovers play at which stadium?
a) Twerton Park   b) Ashton Gate   c) The Memorial Ground

9 Who was Fulham's skipper when they were beaten in the 1975 final by West Ham?
a) Alan Mullery   b) Bobby Moore   c) Alan Ball

10 Brighton reached the final in 1983. Who was their manager that day?
a) Jimmy Melia   b) Graham Taylor   c) David Pleat

The 1927 Cup Final. But who's playing against Arsenal (see question 3)

THE ANSWERS

1b 2c 3c 4b 5a 6a 7b 8c 9a 10a

THE THIRD ROUND OF THE FA CUP

Traditionally, this is the most exciting round of the FA Cup. It's when the teams from the Premiership and Nationwide Division One enter the competition. For the smaller sides it represents an opportunity to mark their name in history with a giant killing, an appearance on Match of the Day and the chance of a bumper payday. There is no other day in the football calender quite like it...

FA Cup Round Three
When the minnows meet the giants

Steve McMahon played in FA Cup finals for Liverpool, but he won't forget the day non-league Stevenage came to Swindon. And Emley almost claimed a Premiership scalp...

Emley's part-timers performed heroics at Upton Park against West Ham before eventually falling to John Hartson's headed winner nine minutes from time. The Unibond League side had matched their millionaire Premiership opponents and even had a chance to take the lead, before Hartson broke their hearts. Although Frank Lampard gave the Irons an early lead, Emley (population 1,800) fought back bravely and

were rewarded for their persistence when Paul David nodded home in the 56th minute. "We did not deserve to win," commented West Ham skipper David Unsworth. "They gave us a lesson in how to pass the ball and played some excellent football," he said.

Arsène Wenger came under fire after his Arsenal side failed to puncture the defence of struggling Nationwide League Port Vale at Highbury. His critics were calling on him to

"I really wanted to win the game but there are important fixtures coming up for us and I have to think about those."
Nottingham Forest manager Dave Bassett, concentrating on the league, after his side were beaten 4-1 at Charlton.

"I always feel I'll be lucky when I play against Everton."
Ian Rush, after his 43rd goal in the FA Cup was enough to beat the team he supported as a boy.

"Thankfully for us, the referee blew for time when the ball was in flight."
Wrexham manager Brian Flynn, after referee Steve Dunn blew for full-time a second before Marcus Gayle headed in for Wimbledon.

rebuild his ageing squad, but the Gunners came through a penalty shoot-out in the replay at Vale Park.

Wigan Athletic staged a late revival but it wasn't enough to stop Roy Hodgson's Blackburn from progressing to the fourth round with a 4-2 win. Despite the defeat, Wigan chairman Dave Whelan was upbeat about their future. "We're spending £31million on a 25,000 seater stadium, and we hope to emulate what Jack Walker has done at Blackburn," said Whelan afterwards.

Sunderland striker Kevin Phillips scored four goals at Milmoor to send Rotherham spinning out of the FA Cup. The former Watford striker, a £350,000 close-season bargain buy for Peter Reid destroyed the South Yorkshire side with a second half hat-trick, this, after converting from the spot early on. "I've scored a hat-trick before but to score four in one game is brilliant," said the four-goal hitman afterwards.

Norwegian striker Jan Aage Fjortoft came off the bench to

THE HIGHEST SCORER IN THE FA CUP

Ian Rush

Rush, Ian James	**TRANSFERS**	**FA CUP GOALS**
Born: **St Asaph 20/10/61**	£300k from Chester in 1980	**Three** for Chester City
Height: **6'0"**	£3.2m to Juventus in 1986	39 in **two** spells at Liverpool
Club honours: **League Div 1, 82,**	£2.8m to Liverpool 1988	**One** for Newcastle
83, 84, 86, 90	Free to Leeds 1996	
League Cup: **81, 82, 83, 84, 95**	Free to Newcastle 1997	
FA Cup: **86, 89, 92**		
European Cup: **84**		

Ian Rush is the all-time highest goal scorer in FA Cup history. He eclipsed Denis Law's record of 41 when he scored his 42nd against Rochdale in 1995 in his second spell at Liverpool. Rush has also scored more goals in FA Cup finals than anyone else – five. He got two against Everton twice! First in 1986, and again in 1989. He also got one against Sunderland in 1992. And he's the top scorer of all-time in domestic competitions with 90 (43 FA Cup, 47 League Cup). Not surprisingly, Rush is the all-time top scorer for Wales.

Chris Sutton tussles with a Wigan Athletic defender in Blackburn's 4-2 victory

Former Liverpool striker Ian Rush is the all-time top scorer in the FA Cup

The story of Round Three...

rescue Sheffield United at Bramall Lane. Fjortoft needed less than 30 seconds to make an impact as he headed in United's equaliser, after Andy Gray had given Bury the lead. Both Gray and Fjortoft scored again in the replay at Gigg Lane but the Blades won by the odd goal to earn a Fourth Round tie at home to Ipswich.

Everton's disappointing season continued when they were beaten by Newcastle at Goodison Park. Worst of all for the Toffeemen, it was an old enemy who inflicted the defeat. Ian Rush, so often a thorn in Everton's side during his glory years with Liverpool, slid home the winner after John Barnes crossed from the byline. It was goal number 26 for Rush against Everton and his 43rd goal in the FA Cup. "I always feel lucky when I play against Everton," said the jubilant Newcastle striker.

Gordon Strachan's much-improved Coventry side came away from Anfield with a deserved 3-1 win. Despite going behind to a fabulous Jamie Redknapp free-kick, the Sky Blues rallied and ended up dominating the game. Darren Huckerby cut in from the left before angling a superb drive past David James before the break and second half goals by Dion Dublin and Paul Telfer ensured Strachan's men a safe passage to the fourth round. But it left Liverpool manager Roy Evans wondering what to do next. "How long can you keep shuffling a disappointing pack?" said the Reds boss.

First Division pacesetters Charlton and Nottingham

"When the ball left the pitch from the corner, the 45 minutes, including all time for stoppages was up."
Referee Steve Dunn's view of the disallowed Wimbledon goal.

"How can you blow when the ball is in the air?"
Joe Kinnear's perspective on the same incident.

"We must do our best for the next six months and see."
Arsène Wenger's cunning plan to frighten Alex Ferguson for the remainder of the season after his team drew a blank at home to Port Vale. Arsenal won the replay on penalties.

Forest met at a rain-sodden Valley, and it was Alan Curbishley's Addicks who progressed to the fourth round with a decisive win. Charlton were two goals to the good by the interval and although Pierre van Hooijdonk, on as a substitute, pulled one back, Carl Leaburn settled the issue before laying one on for Mendonca. Curbishley was pleased with the application of his want-away striker Leaburn, playing on a week-to-week contract: "I don't think Carl wants to leave us," said the Charlton boss. Leaburn joined Wimbledon shortly afterwards.

Darlington's biggest gate of the season saw Wolves ease past the Third Division side to earn a tie against Charlton Athletic. Former Barnet and Crystal Palace hitman Dougie Freedman gave Wolves a first half lead before a brace from Mixu Paatelainen and late strike from Darren Ferguson ensured the Black Country team would be in the hat for the next round.

Controversy raged at Wimbledon when referee Steve Dunn disallowed a late goal by Marcus Gayle which would have sent Wrexham crashing out of the cup. Gayle's header was

TIE OF THE ROUND...

Chelsea 3 Manchester Utd 5

Manchester United and Chelsea were placed first and second in the Premiership on the morning of their Third Round tie, so it was expected to be a closely contested tie between two in-form sides. But United swept Chelsea aside, much to the bemusement of the Stamford Bridge faithful. Indeed, by the time Chelsea woke up, they were 5-0 down, and deservedly so. David Beckham opened the scoring, sliding in from close range before engineering a splendid 30 yard free-kick in off the upright. When Andy Cole scored two superb solo efforts either side of half time, it was all over for the Blues. Late in the game, Le Saux lobbed Schmeichel and Vialli registered twice but the 5-3 scoreline flattered Chelsea. United were in a different class.

David Beckham celebrates Manchester United's opening goal against Chelsea

Teddy Sheringham headed home the fifth goal to knock out holders' Chelsea

The story of Round Three...

flying toward the net as Dunn blew for full-time. The Dons held their nerve in the replay, winning 3-2.

Barnsley narrowly beat fellow Premiership strugglers Bolton 1-0 but the game will be remembered for a mass brawl that involved players, coaching staff, police and stewards. The incident was sparked after Wanderers' defender Neil Cox chased a ball that had gone into touch. The ball landed in the Barnsley dugout and after a little shoving, all hell broke loose. Referee David Elleray claimed he hadn't seen the incident but Match of the Day viewers probably got the best view.

The game? Darren Barnard split the teams with a well executed free-kick in the first half.

In another all-Premiership clash, Derby beat Southampton 2-0 on home turf. The Rams' Italian striker Francesco Baiano converted a hotly-contested spot-kick in the second half to give Derby the lead. Chris Powell settled the issue, rifling the ball into the roof of the net in the 73rd minute.

Australian 'wünderkind' Harry Kewell struck twice in two minutes of the second half against Oxford to ensure Leeds would be in the hat for the Fourth Round. Kewell had tormented the Oxford defence for most of the game but Leeds

"I like a laugh and a joke but sometimes I do the wrong thing and I need to change that."
Darren Huckerby's somewhat sober reflection, after he destroyed Liverpool at Anfield.

"Two things came out of this match. We're out of the cup and Frank Clark is a luckier manager than I am!"
Bradford manager Chris Kamara, after his side were beaten 2-0 by Manchester City. Kamara and City manager Clark were both sacked within weeks.

"We have murdered Aston Villa and Newcastle here, but Emley gave us a much rougher ride."
West Ham's Rio Ferdinand on the Irons' narrow victory over non-league Emley at Upton Park.

were already two goals to the good before the Australian international took centre stage. But Kewell's continual call-ups for the national side were causing his club boss George Graham concern. "I think he will learn more playing in our first team in the Premiership than appearing for Australia in a made-up little competition," said Graham. "A player can always turn round and say he's not playing for his country."

Martin O'Neill's Leicester put four past Northampton at Filbert Street. Ian Marshall opened the Foxes' account before Garry Parker converted a spot-kick. Man of the match Robbie Savage extended Leicester's lead before veteran striker Tony Cottee scored his first goal since his return from a spell in Malaysia. "I am only 32 and I still think I can do it in the Premiership," said Cottee afterwards.

Last season's finalists Middlesbrough progressed to the Fourth Round with a 2-0 win over fellow Division One side QPR. The teams shared four goals in the first game, but Boro booked a glamour date with Arsenal with two second half goals in the replay.

The Fourth Round awaited.

PERFORMANCE OF THE ROUND...

Swindon 1 Stevenage Borough 2

Stevenage Borough pulled off a sensational cup upset at Swindon Town, defeating the shell-shocked First Division side 2-1 at the County Ground. Although Steve McMahon's men took an early lead when Mark Walters struck superbly from 25 yards, they were unable to press home their advantage. Swindon were left rueing missed chances when Jason Soloman rifled in a 23rd minute equaliser, before hero-of-the-hour Giuliano Grazioli slid home what proved to be the winner in the second half. McMahon, so often a winner in his playing career was furious after the game. "Kids would have done better," he blasted. For Stevenage, the victory was vindication for their disappointment at being barred from promotion to the Nationwide League after winning the Conference two seasons ago.

"We've shown in beating Swindon what we would have done in the League."
Borough boss Paul Fairclough

Wimbledon skipper Vinnie Jones led his
side to victory over Wrexham

Mathew Le Tissier couldn't inspire
Southampton to beat Derby County

Round Three results

TIES PLAYED 3/1/98

Arsenal 0	**0 Port Vale**	
	Att: 37,471	

REPLAY 14/1/98 **Port Vale 1**   **1 Arsenal**
Corden 112   Bergkamp 100
Att: 14,964

Arsenal win 4-3 on penalties (aet)

Barnsley 1   **0 Bolton**
Barnard 26   Att: 15,042

Blackburn 4   **2 Wigan**
McGibbon (og) 20   Lee 62
Gallacher 37, 60   Lowe 68
Sherwood 48   Att: 22,402

Bristol Rovers 1   **1 Ipswich**
Beadle 36   Stockwell 71
Att: 8,610

REPLAY 13/1/98 **Ipswich 1**   **0 Bristol Rovers**
Johnson 43   Att: 11,362

Cardiff 1   **0 Oldham**
Fowler 18   Att: 6,635

Charlton 4   **1 Nottingham Forest**
Robinson 38   Van Hooijdonk 56
Brown 42
Leaburn 64
Mendonca 75   Att: 13,827

Crewe 1   **2 Birmingham**
Rivers 31   Furlong 22 (pen) 55
Att: 4,607

Crystal Palace 2   **0 Scunthorpe**
Emblen 45, 87   Att: 11,624

Derby 2   **0 Southampton**
Baiano 68 (pen)
C Powell 73   Att: 27,992

Grimsby 3   **0 Norwich**
McDermott 25
Woods 48
Donovan 76   Att: 8,161

Leeds 4   **0 Oxford**
Radebe 17
Hasselbaink 45 (pen)
Kewell 71, 72   Att: 20,568

Leicester 4   **0 Northampton**
Marshall 17
Parker 26 (pen)
Savage 53
Cottee 58   Att: 20,608

Liverpool 1   **3 Coventry**
Redknapp 7   Huckerby 45
Dublin 62
Telfer 87
Att: 33,888

Manchester City 2   **0 Bradford**
Rosler 35
Brown 42   Att: 23,686

Portsmouth 2   **2 Aston Villa**
Foster 6, 40   Staunton 41
Grayson 88
Att: 16,013

REPLAY 14/1/98 **Aston Villa 1**   **0 Portsmouth**
Milosevic 21   Att: 23,365

Preston 1   **2 Stockport**
Ashcroft 71 (pen)   Angell 30, 48
Att: 12,180

QPR 2   **2 Middlesbrough**
Spencer 6   Hignett 33
Gallen 75   Mustoe 63
Att: 13,379

REPLAY 13/1/98 **Middlesbrough 2**   **0 QPR**
Campbell 54
Mustoe 59   Att: 21,817

Rotherham 1   **5 Sunderland**
Garner 68   Phillips 15 (pen), 55, 72, 76, Quinn 85
Att: 11,500

Leeds striker Harry Kewell celebrates after scoring against Oxford United

Veteran Tony Cottee scored Leicester's fourth as they tonked Northampton 4-0

Round Three results

TIES PLAYED 3/1/98

Sheffield Utd 1	**1 Bury**
Fjortoft 65	Gray 7
	Att: 14,009

REPLAY 13/1/98
Bury 1	**2 Sheffield Utd**
Gray 84	Saunders 48
	Fjortoft 70
	Att: 4,920

Swindon 1	**2 Stevenage**
Walters 6	Soloman 23
	Grazioli 65
	Att: 9,442

Watford 1	**1 Sheffield Wed**
Kennedy 65	Alexandersson 64
	Att: 18,306

REPLAY 14/1/98
Sheffield Wed 0	**0 Watford**
	Att: 18,707

Sheff Wed won 5-3 on penalties aet

West Ham 2	**1 Emley**
Lampard 4	David 56
Hartson 82	Att: 18,629

TIES PLAYED 4/1/98

Chelsea 3	**5 Man Utd**
Le Saux 78	Beckham 23, 28
Vialli 83, 88	Cole 45, 65
	Sheringham 74
	Att: 34,792

Everton 0	**1 Newcastle**
	Rush 67
	Att: 20,885

Wimbledon 0	**0 Wrexham**
	Att: 6,349

REPLAY 13/1/98
Wrexham 2	**3 Wimbledon**
Connolly 7, 46	Hughes 17, 26
	Gayle 35
	Att: 9,539

TIE PLAYED 5/1/98

Tottenham 3	**1 Fulham**
Clemence 20	Smith 54
Calderwood 28	
Taylor 62 (og)	Att: 27,909

13/1/98 (POSTPONED FROM 3/1/98)

AFC Bournemouth 0	**1 Huddersfield Town**
	Stewart 15
	Att: 7,385

Cheltenham 1	**1 Reading**
Watkins 22 (pen)	Morley 71
	Att: 6,000

REPLAY 20/1/98
Reading 2	**1 Cheltenham**
Morley 38	Walker 51
Booty 72	Att: 9,686

Hereford 0	**3 Tranmere**
	Jones 14, 53
	Hill 59
	Att: 7,473

14/1/98 (POSTPONED FROM 3/1/98)

Darlington 0	**4 Wolverhampton**
	Freedman 18
	Paatelainen 66, 87
	Ferguson 90
	Att: 5,018

Portsmouth's Craig Foster scored twice
against Aston Villa, but to no avail

Quiz Two

Test your football knowledge

1 Sutton United beat Coventry City 2-1 in which year?
a) 1988   b) 1989   c) 1990

2 Marcus Stewart scored Huddersfield's winner against Bournemouth in the third round. From which club did he join Town?
a) Bristol City   b) Swindon   c) Bristol Rovers

3 How many times have Sheffield Wednesday won the FA Cup?
a) 4   b) 3   c) 2

4 Ipswich won the cup in 1978. But who scored their winner against Arsenal?
a) Eric Gates   b) Paul Mariner   c) Roger Osborne

5 Peterborough United play at which football ground?
a) Abbey Stadium   b) London Road   c) Sincil Bank

6 Ian Rush is top scorer in the FA Cup with 43 goals. Who is second top scorer?
a) Denis Law   b) Cliff Bastin   c) Peter Osgood

7 Graham Taylor led Watford to the FA Cup Final in which year?
a) 1984   b) 1985   c) 1986

8 To how many FA Cup finals did Brian Clough lead a team?
a) 2   b) never   c) 1

9 Frank Lampard Jnr scored for West Ham against Emley. His dad picked up a winners' medal in 1980 but who did the Hammers beat in the final?
a) QPR   b) Ipswich   c) Arsenal

10 Midfielder Mickey Thomas scored for Wrexham to knock out which Premiership giants in 1992?
a) Tottenham   b) Arsenal   c) Manchester United

What year did Graham Taylor lead Watford to the FA Cup Final? (Question 7)

THE ANSWERS

1 b 2 c 3 b 4 c 5 b 6 a 7 a 8 c 9 c 10 c

THE FOURTH ROUND OF THE FA CUP

This was the round when Stevenage Borough met Newcastle United. Initially, the GM Vauxhall Conference side considered giving up home advantage and moving the tie to St James Park for a bumper payday. But then The Sun newspaper stepped in and sponsored the tie which proved one of the most memorable in the Cup. Certainly, it was the highlight of an otherwise unspectacular round...

FA Cup Round Four

The last of the giantkillers

Stevenage were the only non-league survivors, Cardiff City the only representatives of Nationwide Division Three. And it proved to be the end of the road for both teams...

Two of the Premiership's strugglers, Tottenham Hotspur and Barnsley met at White Hart Lane and Tykes' boss Danny Wilson was the happier of the managers with the 1-1 draw. "We have belief, a great dressing room and a lot of pride," said Wilson. "We defended properly and were more compact." England stopper Sol Campbell gave Spurs the lead before the break but Neil Redfearn levelled from the spot after Clive Wilson had up-ended Ashley Ward. Barnsley finished the job in the replay at Oakwell. Ashley Ward and Neil Redfearn struck for the South Yorkshiremen before David Ginola pulled one back for Spurs. But with the clock ticking down, Darren Barnard engineered a superb drive from 25 yards to guarantee Barnsley a plum Fifth Round tie at Manchester United.

In another all-Premiership clash, Coventry City beat Derby County 2-0 at Highfield Road. Two first half goals from top scorer Dion Dublin silenced the Rams. The Sky Blues' £250,000

Dutchman George Boateng crossed for Dublin to head home eight minutes before the interval, and when Dublin volleyed in Gary Breen's flick right on half-time, there was no way back for Jim Smith's men. Man-of-the-Match Boateng said afterwards: "People think that players in Holland are all flair like Ruud Gullit and Dennis Bergkamp, but there are a lot like me who are hard workers."

Crystal Palace secured their first home win of the season with a 3-0 victory over Premiership rivals Leicester City. Bruce Dyer scored a hat-trick, in direct contrast to Foxes' striker Emile Heskey who failed to convert one of a hatful of opportunities. Steve Coppell was pleased with Dyer's performance but was mystified as to why he cannot do it in the Premiership: "I need him to score on a regular basis," said the Eagles' boss. "I don't want his goals coming like a number 74 bus. They never come on their own, but always in threes."

> **"You just can't stop him and even when we had players around him he just danced past them."**
> West Ham boss Harry Redknapp on their attempts to shackle Georgi Kinkladze.

> **"He could be a Paul Ince."**
> Dion Dublin on Coventry team mate George Boateng.

> **"We have belief, a great dressing room and a lot of pride."**
> Danny Wilson after his Barnsley side overcame Spurs.

Roy Hodgson's in-form Blackburn Rovers impressed in the Monday televised game, beating Sheffield Wednesday 3-0 at Hillsborough. A crowd of just 15,940 turned up to see Rovers triumph over Ron Atkinson's disappointing Owls. Chris Sutton volleyed in from close range in the sixth minute before skipper Tim Sherwood started and finished a superb move eight minutes before the interval. Young Republic of Ireland winger Damien Duff capped a fine performance with a stunning individual strike in the last minute. Duff lobbed the ball over a Wednesday defender and fashioned a fine volley in the bottom corner past Kevin Pressman.

City rivals Sheffield United fared better than their Wednesday counterparts, although the Blades needed a replay to beat Nationwide rivals Ipswich Town. Dean Saunders equalised David Johnson's strike at Portman Road before Don Hutchison converted a penalty in the replay at Bramall Lane to ensure United's

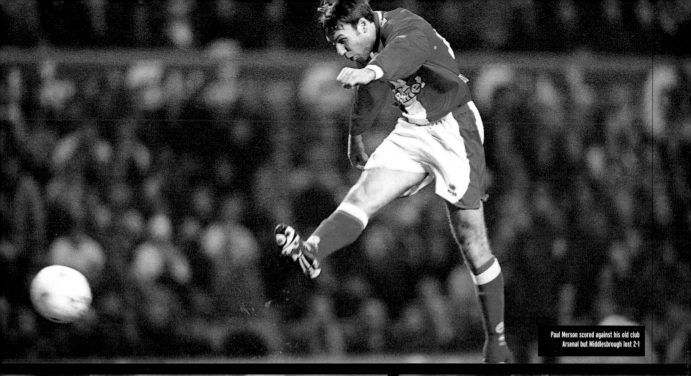

Paul Merson scored against his old club
Arsenal but Middlesbrough lost 2-1

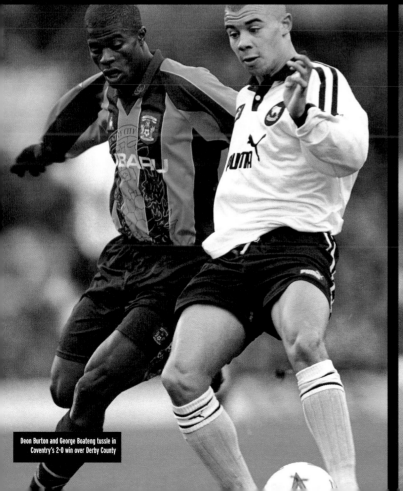

Deon Burton and George Boateng tussle in
Coventry's 2-0 win over Derby County

Andy Cole scored twice as Manchester
United thrashed Walsall 5-1 at home

The story of Round Four...

TIE OF THE ROUND...

One tie above all others dominated the Fourth Round of the FA Cup. Stevenage Borough of the GM Vauxhall Conference were drawn against mighty Newcastle United and the publicity the match generated was immense. At first, Stevenage had considered swapping the tie from their home ground to St James Park, where a 36,000 gate would have guaranteed the non-league team extra revenue. But then The Sun newspaper stepped in and sponsored the Conference side, ensuring that they could play at Broadhall Way and earn a substantial purse from the tie. Temporary stands were erected to house extra fans but this led to Newcastle boss Kenny Dalglish questioning safety at the ground. Borough chairman Victor Green was incensed at the comments, and an ugly slanging match ensued. The publicity didn't reflect well on Newcastle and Dalglish, not known for his personable demeanour, appeared more mealy-mouthed than ever. But Dalglish was obviously concerned about fans' safety.

The match was televised on a bitterly cold Sunday afternoon and it marked Alan Shearer's first start since his return from injury.

Ominously for Stevenage, it didn't take long for the England hitman to register. In the third minute, Keith Gillespie was released down the right and his pinpoint cross was headed home by Shearer at the far post. Lesser teams than Stevenage would have crumbled but it only increased the resolve of the Hertfordshire side. Two minutes before the interval, Stevenage won a corner and from Gary Crawshaw's cross, Giuliano Grazioli sneaked in between two defenders to head home. The match finished 1-1, much to relief of Newcastle. "It was a very difficult game and the conditions favoured them," said Dalglish.

The teams met again 10 days later at St James Park in front of 36,705, the biggest day in Stevenage's history. And again, Alan Shearer gave Newcastle the lead, slotting in from close range on 16 minutes. The England striker extended the Magpies' lead midway through the second half, but television pictures later showed that Stevenage defender Mark Smith had cleared before the whole of the ball crossed the line. Gary Crawshaw gave the visitors hope with a goal in the 74th minute but it wasn't to be for Paul Fairclough's men.

> "They gave everything out there, I'm so proud of them. Now we've got to make sure that we play just as well in the Conference"
> Stevenage Borough boss Paul Fairclough after the game.

> "At the start of the game, Stan Collymore and myself gave each other high fives."
> Dwight Yorke describes his pre-match bonding ritual with his strike partner, after Aston Villa had beaten West Brom 4-0.

> "Sometimes the English players are not as honest as they would like us to believe they are. Maybe they watch too much Italian football on TV."
> Middlesbrough's Italian defender Gianluca Festa postulates on English football, after the 2-1 reverse at home to Arsenal.

> "All he wants to be now is Sylvester Stallone."
> Walsall striker Roger Boli on fellow countryman Eric Cantona's new acting career.

progress. Hutchison later joined former Blades' boss Howard Kendall at Everton.

Manchester City's brief respite from their dismal league form ended in defeat at home to West Ham United. Despite a virtuoso performance from Georgian midfielder Georgi Kinkladze, the Hammers secured victory when former City man Steve Lomas slotted in the winner 15 minutes from the end. It was cruel luck on Frank Clark's men, who should have taken the lead minutes before Lomas struck, when Paul Dickov was brought down in the box by Steve Potts. But City's German striker Uwe Rosler smacked the resultant spot kick high and wide. Eyel Berkovic put West Ham ahead in the first half before Kinkladze brought Maine Road to its feet with a brilliant equaliser on the hour. The Georgian cut in from the left and jinked past three West Ham defenders before firing a brilliant shot in off the post. But when Rosler missed the penalty, Frank Clark knew it wasn't to be his day. "To miss from the spot is not really a case of bad luck," he admitted. "But maybe this game sums up our season perfectly." For Clark,

Paul Fairclough, the Stevenage manager was proud of his team's performance...

...and chairman Victor Green was even more pleased with the revenue

Stevenage fans were quick to congratulate new-found hero Guiliano Grazioli

The story of Round Four...

though, it was almost the end of the road. He was eventually replaced by Joe Royle but City's season ended in ignominy when they were relegated to the Second Division for the first time in their history. Next season, their local derby is not with neighbours United, but with Macclesfield Town.

Aston Villa comfortably triumphed over West Bromwich Albion in the West Midlands' derby at Villa Park. Dwight Yorke claimed a brace in between strikes from Simon Grayson and Stan Collymore. West Brom skipper Richard Sneekes was impressed with Yorke. "You can see why he is worth £10m – he would be worth every penny at that price." There was no place in the Villa line-up for Savo

Milosevic, after he had spat at Villa fans during their game at Ewood Park against Blackburn the week previously. Milosevic stayed on until the end of the season and then switched to Real Zaragoza for £3.7million.

Charlton Athletic's match against fellow Nationwide League Division One side Wolverhampton Wanderers ended 1-1 at the Valley. However, Mark McGhee's men proved the stronger in the replay at Molineux, winning decisively by three goals. Keith Curle scored a first half penalty before Stuart Naylor and Mixu Paatelainen secured Wolves a Fifth Round tie at Selhurst Park against Wimbledon.

Middlesbrough's Paul Merson was pitted against his old Arsenal team-mates when

> **"The pitch didn't suit our passing game."**
> Peter Reid's verdict after Tranmere beat Sunderland at Prenton Park.

> **"Newcastle did not show us enough respect."**
> Stevenage Borough's Giuliano Grazioli after the 1-1 draw against the Geordies.

> **"We respected Stevenage before the game and we will do the same in the replay."**
> Kenny Dalglish on the Conference side. Newcastle narrowly won the replay 2-1.

> **"Mr Graham can be very hard at times. You have to try to perform to your best and show him you deserve to be in the side."**
> Jimmy Floyd Hasselbaink's verdict on his manager.

the Gunners visited the Riverside. Arsene Wenger's men set off like a steam train, Marc Overmars sprinting through a static Middlesbrough defence to shoot them into a first minute lead. The majority of the 28,264 crowd were left stunned when Ray Parlour ran onto a pass from Nicolas Anelka to extend the Gunners' lead. Arsenal wasted chance after chance before Merson gave Middlesbrough hope, finishing from 25 yards after Alex Manninger had unwisely emerged from his 18 yard area. But Arsenal were good value for their 2-1 win, and Arsene Wenger was pleased with the performance: "For 45 minutes, I thought we were very impressive and we played some great football." For the Gunners, it was the start of a run that would lead them to a possible domestic double. Paul Merson was disappointed not to put one over his old club, but recognised that the league was more important: "Arsenal slaughtered us in the first half. We made a lot of schoolboy errors and the way it was going I would have settled to lose by six. But we should be proud of ourselves for the way we played in the second half. If

STEVENAGE BOROUGH CLUB DETAILS

Stevenage Borough	**Formed:** 1976
Home: Broadhall Way	**Chairman:** Victor Green
Capacity: 3,700	**Manager:** Paul Fairclough

Stevenage Borough were this season's biggest non-league story in the FA Cup. But they could well have been a Nationwide League club by now. Borough won the GM Vauxhall Conference in 1996 but were denied promotion because their ground facilities were not up to scratch by the cut-off date. Despite a protracted court battle based on the fact that the ground would be ready in time for the next season, the bid failed.

Manager Paul Fairclough is regarded as one of the most successful managers in non-league. He lead Borough from the Isthmian League Division 2 to first in the GM Conference in five seasons.

Mark Bright of Charlton was dismissed against Wolverhampton Wanderers

Peter Reid's Sunderland were beaten by Tranmere despite his shouting

Joe Kinnear's Wimbledon narrowly beat Huddersfield at the McAlpine Stadium

The story of Round Four...

we play like that throughout every game in the rest of the season, then we will go up." And he added: "It would have been an extra game at Arsenal and that's the last thing we needed. So it's better for us that the cup tie was concluded on the day. It would have been nice to have won it, but the biggest disappointment for me was that Nottingham Forest won at QPR." Depite that result Bryan Robson's men held on to Forest's shirt tails and claimed the second automatic promotion place.

Manchester United put five past Nationwide Division Two side Walsall at Old Trafford. Andy Cole and Ole Solskjaer helped themselves to two goals apiece and Ronnie Johnsen scored the fifth after Walsall's French hitman Roger Boli had put the Midlanders on the score sheet. Boli was ecstatic with his goal, despite the 5-1 defeat: "To score here was for me a dream I couldn't have imagined," he said afterwards.

Leeds United eased past Grimsby Town with a comfortable 2-0 victory at Elland Road. And it was a case of 'Double Dutch' for United. Central defender Robert Molenaar headed home Gary

Kelly's corner on the stroke of half-time, before top scorer Jimmy Floyd Hasselbaink lashed in a drive from just inside the box to make the tie safe. Leeds manager George Graham was pleased with the performance of his £2m striker: "There is no question he has the strength to be effective in English football, " said Graham. "He has that quality all top strikers need – total self confidence." Hasselbaink continued his rich vein of form for the remainder of the season and was later chosen in the final 22 for the Dutch World Cup squad.

Wimbledon overcame a potentially tricky hurdle at Huddersfield Town. Dons midfielder Neil Ardley scored the only goal of the game at the McAlpine Stadium, with a crashing 20 yard drive in the 62nd minute. Wayne Allison should have equalised for Town but Wimbledon hung on to secure a tie at home to Wolves.

Elsewhere, Tranmere Rovers beat high-flying Sunderland, teenager Andy Parkinson's goal eliminating Peter Reid's men. "The pitch didn't suit our passing game," quipped Reid. It left Sunderland to concentrate their efforts on

"Wimbledon were lucky against us and they were lucky in the last round against Wrexham."

Huddersfield's Barry Horne in magnanimous mood after their 1-0 defeat.

"That performance was so typical of Bruce – brilliant one minute, awful the next. But that's his appeal."

Steve Coppell on Crystal Palace striker Bruce Dyer after his hat-trick against Leicester.

"I feel as though we have been knocked out."

A relieved Trevor Francis after his Birmingham charges were almost caught out by nine-man Stockport.

gaining an automatic promotion spot. Unfortunately for Reid, Sunderland came in third and had to settle for a place in the play-offs.

Another all-First Division tie saw Birmingham City overcome Stockport County, who were left with nine men by the end of the game. Bryan Hughes scored twice for City, while Middlesbrough-bound Alun Armstrong registered for Stockport. County boss Gary Megson was critical of referee Gary Willard's handling of the match: "If he's a Premiership referee, then give me Nationwide League officials," fumed Megson.

Reading progressed to the Fifth Round, but needed a reply and a penalty shoot-out to beat Third Division Cardiff City. In the first tie at Ninian Park, Kevin Nugent gave the Welshmen a 1-0 lead two minutes after the interval but Carl Asaba equalised to ensure a replay. At Elm Park, City went into the interval a goal to the good before former Manchester City striker Trevor Morley struck Reading's equaliser. Extra time couldn't separate the teams but Reading prevailed in the penalty shoot-out.

Kevin Pressman of Wednesday can't keep out Chris Sutton's strike for Blackburn

Steve Lomas celebrates scoring the winner for West Ham against Manchester City

FA Cup

Round Four results

Aston Villa 4   **0 West Bromwich Albion**
Grayson 4
Yorke 62, 64
Collymore 72   Att: 39,372

Birmingham City 2   **1 Stockport County**
Hughes 32, 84   Armstrong 66
   Att: 15,882

Cardiff City 1   **1 Reading**
Nugent 47   Asaba 56
Att: 10,174

REPLAY 3/2/98   **Reading 1**   **1 Cardiff City**
Morley 56   Dale 40
   Att: 11,808
Reading won 4-3 on penalties aet

Charlton Athletic 1   **1 Wolverhampton**
Jones 64   Richards 47
   Att: 15,540

REPLAY 3/2/98   **Wolverhampton 3**   **0 Charlton Athletic**
Curle 29 (pen)
Naylor 48
Paatelainen 65   Att: 20,429

Coventry City 2   **0 Derby County**
Dublin 38, 45   Att: 22,864

Crystal Palace 3   **0 Leicester City**
Dyer 33, 62, 66   Att: 15,489

Huddersfield Town 0   **1 Wimbledon**
   Ardley 62
   Att: 14,533

Ipswich Town 1   **1 Sheffield Utd**
Johnson 45   Saunders 82
   Att: 14,654

REPLAY 3/2/98   **Sheffield Utd 1**   **0 Ipswich Town**
Hutchison 13 pen   Att: 14,144

Leeds United 2   **0 Grimsby Town**
Molenaar 45
Hasselbaink 79   Att: 29,598

Manchester Utd 5   **1 Walsall**
Cole 10, 65   Boli 72
Solskjaer 39, 68
Johnson 74   Att: 54,669

Middlesbrough 1   **2 Arsenal**
Merson 62   Overmars 1
Parlour 19
   Att: 28,264

Tottenham 1   **1 Barnsley**
Campbell 30   Redfearn 59 pen
   Att: 28,722

REPLAY 2/2/98   **Barnsley 3**   **1 Tottenham**
Ward 50   Ginola 72
Redfearn 58
Barnard 88   Att: 18,220

Tranmere 1   **0 Sunderland**
Parkinson 77   Att: 14,055

Manchester City 1   **2 West Ham**
Kinkladze 59   Berkovic 28
Lomas 76
   Att: 26,495

Stevenage Borough 1   **1 Newcastle**
Grazioli 42   Shearer 3
   Att: 8,040

REPLAY 2/2/98   **Newcastle 2**   **1 Stevenage**
Shearer 16, 65   Crawshaw 74
   Att: 36,705

Sheffield Wednesday 0   **3 Blackburn**
   Sutton 6
Sherwood 37
Duff 87
   Att: 15,940

Lee Hendrie controls the ball in Aston Villa's 4-0 victory over West Brom

Carl Asaba scored for Reading in their first game against Cardiff City

Christian Gross couldn't inspire Tottenham Hotspur to victory against Barnsley

Quiz Three
Test your football knowledge

1 Colchester's Fifth Round defeat of Leeds United in 1971 is regarded as the biggest cup upset ever. What score was it?
a) 2-1   b) 1-0   c) 3-2

2 Paul Merson scored for Middlesbrough against Arsenal this season but who were Arsenal playing when he picked up a winners' medal in 1993?
a) Sunderland   b) Sheffield Wednesday   c) Liverpool

3 Coventry manager Gordon Strachan has how many winners' medals?
a) 3   b) 2   c) 1

4 In which county of England is Stevenage Borough?

a) Buckinghamshire   b) Bedfordshire   c) Hertfordshire

5 Who skippered Manchester City to the cup in 1969?
a) Tony Book b)   Colin Bell   c) Mike Summerbee

6 How many times have Leeds United reached the FA Cup final?
a) 4   b) 5   c) 6

7 Apart from this year, when did Newcastle last reach an FA Cup final?
a) 1974   b) 1975   c) 1976

8 Which former Everton boss played in the 1966 final when the Toffees beat Sheffield Wednesday 3-2?
a) Howard Kendal   b) Joe Royle   c) Colin Harvey

9 Who was manager of Manchester United when they beat Liverpool 2-1 in the 1977 FA Cup final?
a) Dave Sexton   b) Tommy Docherty   c) Wilf McGuinness

10 Chelsea won the FA Cup in 1970, but who did they beat in the European Cup Winners' Cup final in 1971?
a) Valencia   b) Real Madrid   c) Barcelona

Paul Merson got a winners' medal in 1993. Against which team? (Question 2)

THE ANSWERS

1c 2b 3a 4c 5a 6c 7a 8c 9b 10b

THE FIFTH ROUND OF THE FA CUP

The 304 teams that entered the FA Cup are reduced to just 16 by the Fifth Round. Nine-times winners Manchester United fell at this hurdle to lowly Barnsley and the other teams breathed a collective sigh of relief. Wolverhampton Wanderers caused the only other upset of the round, beating Wimbledon in a replay at Molineux. And the fans started to dream of a trip to the Twin Towers...

5TH ROUND (REPLAY)

Crystal Palace 1   Arsenal 2

Dyer 35   Anelka 2, Bergkamp 28

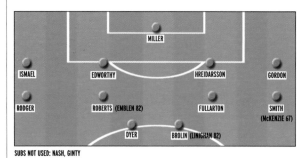

SUBS NOT USED: NASH, GINTY

SUBS NOT USED: LUKIC, RANKIN, VERNAZZA

After a stalemate at Highbury, notable for two obvious penalties which the referee waved away, Arsenal overcame Crystal Palace at Selhurst Park...   Att: 15,674 Ref: M J Bodenham

Arsenal's FA Cup clash at Highbury against Crystal Palace ended in a disappointing stalemate. But the match will remain in the memory for two astonishing decisions by referee Martin Bodenham, who dismissed penalty appeals by both teams. In the 42nd minute, Arsenal keeper Alex Manninger, deputising for the injured David Seaman, up-ended Jamie Fullerton inside the box. Manninger received the yellow card and Palace were awarded a free-kick outside the box, much to their disbelief. "If it was in the box, and it appeared to be, then it was a penalty," said Arsene Wenger, afterwards. But he added: "I'm not scared about Manninger

and the way he comes out for a ball – he doesn't concede goals and with luck, he'll be a great keeper." Later, when Steve Bould's pass released Stephen Hughes, the Arsenal youngster was brought down in the box by Andy Roberts. Referee Bodenham, whom Alex Ferguson has claimed sees nothing, waved play on. "They were both penalties," conceded Palace boss Steve Coppell afterwards.

The replay was set against the backdrop of Mark Goldberg's protracted £30million takeover bid of Crystal Palace, and his attempts to land Terry Venables as successor to Steve Coppell.

Did you know? Crystal Palace spent £12m in the transfer market when they were promoted to the Premiership but still got relegated

This, of course, meant nothing to Arsenal's in-form teenage striker Nicolas Anelka who took just two minutes to puncture the Palace rearguard. Dennis Bergkamp fashioned a defence-splitting pass and Anelka calmly lobbed the advancing Kevin Miller. Bergkamp extended the Gunners' lead on the half hour, though he was fortunate to see his shot deflect off a Palace defender. Bruce Dyer pulled one back for Palace before the break, touching home Thomas Brolin's flick-on from close range, but Palace's task was made impossible when Dean Gordon was dismissed for pulling back Anelka.

FIRST MATCH	REPLAY			
Sunday 15 February Att: 37,164 Ref: M J Bodenham	**2 minutes:**	**28 minutes:**	**35 minutes:**	**61 minutes:**
Arsenal (0) 0	Anelka latches onto Bergkamp's	Dennis Bergkamp extends Arsenal's	Bruce Dyer halves the deficit, firing in	Manninger denies Dyer an equaliser
Crystal Palace (0) 0	through-ball and lobs over Miller (1-0)	lead when his shot deflects off	from 10 yards (2-1)	with a fine save
The referee that Manchester United manager Alex Ferguson claims "sees	26 minutes: Dean Gordon is sent off	Edworthy (2-0)		
nothing" took centre stage, dismissing two obvious penalty appeals. Martin	for pulling back Anelka			
Bodenham waved away claims from Stephen Hughes and Jamie Fullerton.				

Dennis Bergkamp forces his way through
the Crystal Palace defence

5TH ROUND

Aston Villa 0

Coventry City 1

Moldovan 72

SUBS NOT USED: NELSON, OATES, WALKER, COLLINS

SUBS NOT USED: JOHANSEN, HAWORTH, OGRIZOVIC

Coventry City had never won at Villa Park in their history. But under Gordon Strachan the Sky Blues were in the form of their lives when they met Aston Villa...

Att: 36,979 Ref: G S Willard

Coventry City, who destroyed Liverpool at Anfield in the previous round, had never won at Villa Park in their history, but the hoodoo was smashed when City's Romanian international Viorel Moldovan fired home a second half winner. Gordon Strachan's men thoroughly deserved their victory over a lacklustre Aston Villa side which desperately missed the presence of leading goalscorer Dwight Yorke. Stan Collymore lead the front line but created few opportunities for strikes on goal.

Coventry should have made the game safe long before Moldovan struck and Norwegian midfielder Trond Soltvedt could well have helped himself to a hat-trick. In the 22nd minute, Soltvedt struck a powerful shot from the edge of the box which looked certain to beat Mark Bosnich after it took a deflection off Villa defender Ugo Ehiogu. But the Villa keeper adjusted his body in mid-air and miraculously volleyed clear with his trailing leg in one of the most memorable saves of the season. The Norwegian steered another shot just wide of the upright on half-time and he came even closer after the break, only to see Julian Joachim clear his net-bound strike off the line.

Did you know?
Viorel Moldovan's son is named Gianluca after Chelsea boss and former Juventus striker Gianluca Vialli

In the 58th minute Strachan made a tactical switch which changed the game. Richard Shaw was consigned to the bench, Dion Dublin moved to central defence and City's record £3.25million signing Viorel Moldovan joined Darren Huckerby in the forward line. Soon after, George Boateng skipped past three Villa defenders and although Bosnich palmed away the Dutchman's shot, Moldovan swept in the rebound from close range. "It was nice to create a bit of history," was Strachan's verdict. Villa boss Brian Little was replaced by his former coach John Gregory soon after.

KEY MOMENTS

22nd minute:
Trond Soltvedt's deflected shot is brilliantly volleyed away by Mark Bosnich, after the Villa keeper adjusts his body in mid-air

58th minute:
Viorel Moldovan enters the fray and Dublin reverts to central defence

64th minute:
Another good Soltvedt strike is cleared off the line by Julian Joachim

71st minute:
George Boateng's close range effort is palmed away by Bosnich, only for Moldovan to steer home the winner from close range

Gordon Strachan congratulates Coventry
City goalscorer Viorel Moldovan

5TH ROUND

Leeds United 3
Wallace 5, Hasselbaink 28, 87

Birmingham City 2
Ablett 63, Ndlovu 81

SUBS NOT USED: MATTHEWS, McPHAIL, SHEPHERD, BEENEY

SUBS NOT USED: FORINTON, HOLLAND, POOLE

Leeds tie with Birmingham was their third at home against lower league opposition in the cup this season. And Trevor Francis' men gave them an almighty scare...

Att: 35,463 Ref: D J Gallagher

Leeds won a match that could so easily have slipped from their grasp after Birmingham battled back from a 2-0 half-time deficit. The Nationwide League side struck twice after the interval to cancel out goals from Rod Wallace and Jimmy Floyd Hasselbaink, only for Hasselbaink to break their hearts with a controversial winner three minutes from the death.

No-one could have guessed that it would be so close after the way Leeds tore into Trevor Francis's men in the first half. Birmingham's central defensive partnership of Steve Bruce and Gary Ablett were given a torrid time in the first 45 minutes by the pace and power of Leeds' front two. In the fifth minute, Rod Wallace outpaced the Blues' defence and finished with clinical precision from 10 yards. Then Hasselbaink played a superb one-two with strike partner Wallace, before catching out Ian Bennett at the near post with a powerful left foot drive. But Leeds couldn't add to their tally before the break.

Gary Ablett pulled one back for the Blues, heading home John McCarthy's corner at the near post and, in the 81st minute, Peter Ndlovu silenced the majority of the 35,463 crowd when he fired the equaliser past Nigel Martyn.

Did you know?
The West Stand at Elland Road is being rebuilt this summer at a cost of £10million. Once complete, the capacity will rise to 45,000.

Leeds rallied and when Lee Bowyer was up-ended on the edge of the box, Hasselbaink rose above his marker John McCarthy to head home Bruno Ribeiro's free-kick. McCarthy complained he had been impeded but the ref allowed the goal to stand.

It was another cup defeat for Trevor Francis at the hands of George Graham. Francis steered Sheffield Wednesday to two Wembley finals against Arsenal in 1993, but the Gunners lifted the silverware on both occasions. "This defeat hurts, but George's teams are always well organised and difficult to breakdown," conceded the Birmingham boss.

KEY MOMENTS

5 minutes:
Rod Wallace outpaces Steve Bruce and slides the ball past Bennett

28 minutes:
Hasselbaink plays clever one-two with Wallace and drives in left foot shot

63 minutes:
Ablett heads in at the near post from McCarthy's centre

81 minutes:
Ndlovu bursts clear and shoots past Nigel Martyn from 20 yards

87 minutes:
Hasselbaink heads home Ribeiro's free-kick to win the tie

Leeds players congratulate Rod Wallace
after his spectacular opening goal

5TH ROUND (REPLAY)

Barnsley 3

Hendrie 9, Jones 45, 65

Manchester United 2

Sheringham 56, Cole 81

SUBS NOT USED: TINKLER, HRISTOV

SUBS NOT USED: VAN DER GOUW, CASPER

This match was bottom of the Premiership versus top. But Danny Wilson's men were made of much sterner stuff than at the start of the season...

Att: 18,655 Ref: M A Riley

Without a shadow of a doubt, Barnsley's clash with Manchester United was the tie of the round. Despite the fact that the Yorkshiremen won the replay at Oakwell 3-2, many felt that Danny Wilson's men were denied a clear-cut penalty in the first tie at Old Trafford which should have secured their passage without a replay. Barnsley substitute Andy Liddell was felled by a knee-high challenge from Gary Neville six minutes from time, only for referee Mike Riley to wave away Liddell's claims. Earlier in the game, United goalkeeper Peter Schmeichel had gifted Barnsley the lead with an uncharacteristic error. The Danish

international skewed a back-pass and the ball spun into the path of John Hendrie who stole in to finish neatly. Four minutes later, United conjured up an equaliser for Teddy Sheringham with a neat passing move, and the former Tottenham striker slotted home from six yards.

In the replay, Alex Ferguson, as expected, rested members of his first team in anticipation of United's forthcoming Champions' League clash against Monaco. Despite their weakened side, United remained the favourites but they were not prepared for the intensity and

> **Did you know?**
> Barnsley took 8,000 fans to Old Trafford for the first leg, their biggest support away from home ever

commitment of a rejuvenated Barnsley. Hendrie gave the Tykes a lead on nine minutes with a superb strike which flew into the top corner of the net. Right on half-time, rookie defender Scott Jones extended Barnsley's lead. Ferguson introduced Teddy Sheringham, who brought United within reach when he latched onto a ball from Andy Cole to convert from eight yards. Scott Jones restored Barnsley's two-goal advantage with a towering header before Cole gave the champions hope on 81 minutes. Despite a frantic finish, United couldn't scrape an equaliser and Barnsley strode on to the last eight.

FIRST MATCH	REPLAY			
Sunday 15 February Att: 53,700 Ref: Michael Riley **Manchester United (1) 1** Sheringham 42 **Barnsley (1) 1** Hendrie 38 John Hendrie gave the Tykes a shock lead when Peter Schmeichel sliced the ball towards his own net. Barnsley should have had a penalty at the death when Gary Neville took out Andy Liddell at knee height.	**45 minutes:** Scott Jones scores Barnsley's second to give them 2-0 half time lead	**56 minutes:** Sheringham reduces deficit after Cole steps over a Beckham cross and leaves it to Teddy	**65 minutes:** Jones heads his second and Barnsley's third from Barnard's cross	**81 minutes:** Cole gives United hope but Barnsley hold on

Teddy Sheringham scored in both ties but
Manchester United were defeated

5TH ROUND

Newcastle United 1   Tranmere Rovers 0

Shearer 22

SUBS NOT USED: HISLOP, PEACOCK, RUSH

SUBS NOT USED: POWELL, MAHON

After rescuing Newcastle United from an embarrassing situation against Stevenage Borough, Alan Shearer was the hero once again for Kenny Dalglish's side...

Att: 36,675 Ref: G R Ashby

Newcastle United put their dismal season behind them to secure a berth in the last eight of the FA Cup thanks to Alan Shearer. The England man struck his fourth Cup goal of the season, but a sub-standard Newcastle performance did little to suggest that the Geordies could turn their season around. Kenny Dalglish's side struggled to overcome Tranmere in a rather grim encounter at St James Park, and it was First Division Rovers who played most of the positive football.

However, once again it was Shearer who was the difference between Newcastle and their opponents. The £15million striker who'd rescued

Newcastle against Stevenage in the previous round, was on hand to head home a cross from Alessandro Pistone in the 22nd minute. It was Shearer's fourth headed goal of Newcastle's Cup campaign and it illustrated how indispensable he is to them. "All the goals I've scored so far have been headers and they've all been pretty similar," said Shearer afterwards. He added: "The FA Cup is our only chance of silverware this season and if we get a bit of luck in the draw we might just do something."

Tranmere had a number of opportunities and could have gone

Did you know?
When Kenny Dalglish was Liverpool manager, he signed Tranmere boss John Aldridge as a replacement for Ian Rush

ahead as early as the 14th minute, when Clint Hill met John Morrissey's centre only to see the ball rebound off Shay Given's legs. Former Newcastle striker David Kelly saw his header cleared off the line by Pistone just before the break, and then Given palmed over a fierce John McGreal drive. But Newcastle were not to be denied and held on to the end. Former Toon striker David Kelly thought that Newcastle were lucky. "They were spawny against Stevenage and they were spawny against us," he said after the match. "They had one chance and they won 1-0."

KEY MOMENTS

14 minutes:
Clint Hill's strike forces a good save from Shay Given

22 minutes:
Alan Shearer heads home Alessandro Pistone's magnificent centre ball to give Newcastle the lead

30 minutes:
Pistone clears a David Kelly header off the line

37 minutes:
Tranmere keeper Simonson produces a fine save from Robert Lee

61 minutes:
Given tips John McGreal's long range effort over the bar

England skipper Alan Shearer was once again Newcastle United's match-winner

FA CUP WINNERS

49

5TH ROUND

Sheffield United 1   Reading 0

Sandford 87

Sheffield United:
KELLY
BORBOKIS — SANDFORD — HOLDSWORTH — QUINN
FORD — MARKER — HUTCHISON — STUART (MARCELO 76)
TAYLOR — SAUNDERS (KATCHOURO 89)

SUBS NOT USED: KELLY, BEARD, BURLEY

Reading:
BIBBO
BOOTY — SWALES — BERNAL — PRIMUS
PARKINSON — BOWEN — HOUGHTON — HODGES
MORLEY — ASABA (WILLIAMS 83)

SUBS NOT USED: McPHERSON, ASHDOWN, MEAKER, LOVELL

Nigel Spackman was still at the helm when the Blades met fellow Nationwide Division One side Reading at Bramall Lane. And United secured a comfortable passage...   Att: 17,845 Ref: N S Barry

Friday the 13th proved lucky for Sheffield United as the Blades progressed to the Quarter-finals with a narrow victory over Reading. It was just reward for a spirited performance by Nigel Spackman's men who dominated throughout. Poor Reading didn't manage a single strike on goal in the whole of the 90 minutes. With Earl Barrett cup-tied and Roger Nilsen injured, Spackman played three centre-halves and brought in Vas Borbokis and Wayne Quinn as wing-backs to give the Blades extra width.

United almost scored in the first minute when Dean Saunders struck from 12 yards out, only for the ball to rebound off the bar. Soon after, Vas Borbokis almost engineered an opening for former-Everton midfielder Graham Stuart who just failed to connect. Then Blades' striker Gareth Taylor almost capitalised on a great ball from Ford, but Reading keeper Sal Bibbo smothered the ball at his feet. Before the interval two more chances fell to Reading: first Asaba and then Trevor Morley blasted wide. It was brief respite for Reading though, as United found another gear. Bibbo tipped Saunders' low, angled drive onto an upright and then Graeme Stuart whipped Quinn's cross just over.

Did you know?
Sheffield United won the cup in 1925 after an error by Cardiff City defender Harry Wake. One Welsh newspaper headline read: 'Wake Not Awake'.

After the break, United dominated possession but couldn't find the key to unlock the Reading defence. Saunders and Stuart were both wasteful, and the closest Spackman's men came to a goal was when Reading centre-half Andy Bernal headed a Borbokis centre onto his own woodwork. Brazilian striker Marcelo replaced Graham Stuart and almost made an immediate impact, only to be denied by a point-blank stop from Bibbo. Then, with the clock ticking down, Vas Borbokis sped down the right and his centre was met by a flying header from Lee Sandford at the far post; 1-0. Game over.

KEY MOMENTS

1 minute:
Dean Saunders rattles the bar with a vicious 12 yard strike

24 minutes:
Reading keeper Sal Bibbo denies Gareth Taylor, smothering the ball at the striker's feet

48 minutes:
Reading defender Andy Bernal heads against his own bar from a Vas Borbokis centre

87 minutes:
Lee Sandford heads in the winner from close range after a jinking run and neat cross from wing-back Borbokis

5TH ROUND (REPLAY)

Blackburn Rovers 1   West Ham United 1

Ripley 114

Hartson 103

SUBS NOT USED: BROOMES, STEWART

SUBS NOT USED: BREAKER, POTTS, BISHOP, LAMA

A 2-2 draw, a flying elbow, a sending off – and that was just the first game. Roy Hodgson and Harry Redknapp pleaded for calm in the replay...

Att: 21,972 Ref: P Jones

West Ham progressed to the last eight after skipper Steve Lomas struck the crucial spot-kick in a penalty shoot-out at Ewood Park. It was the culmination of a mammoth battle against Blackburn Rovers which began 10 days earlier in a stormy game at Upton Park. Here, controversy surrounded the dismissal of Kevin Gallacher for elbowing Eyal Berkovic, whose theatrical dive angered many Rovers players. But Roy Hodgson's side rallied with 10 men and salvaged a draw when Chris Sutton headed home in the second half. "When they're down to 10 men, we have to go in and kill them off," said Hammers boss Harry

Redknapp after the first tie. And he added: "We shouldn't be going to Ewood Park for a replay – it should have been over today." Rovers boss Hodgson was more concerned that the controversy surrounding Gallacher's dismissal shouldn't spread ill-feeling amongst his players in the replay. "If there is any bitterness with regard to any West Ham player, it's imperative I speak to the players concerned," he said. "It's vital we try to beat them as football team and that we don't start trying to wreak any revenge for anything that people think has happened here."

Did you know?
Mervyn Day, who played in goal for West Ham when they beat Fulham in the 1975 FA Cup final, is now goalkeeping coach at Everton

And so to Ewood Park. Both teams had their chances but at the end of the 90 minutes, the score was 0-0. However, when John Hartson controlled the ball with his chest and swept the ball past Alan Fettis in the 104th minute, Redknapp must have thought his side had won it. But 10 minutes later, Stuart Ripley's rare header brought the sides level, and it edged the game into a nerve-wracking penalty shoot-out. Unfortunately for Rovers, Colin Hendry's spot kick was saved by the legs of Craig Forrest and then Lomas converted to send West Ham into the Quarter-finals.

FIRST MATCH	REPLAY	West Ham win 5-4 on penalties after extra time

FIRST MATCH

Saturday 14 February   Att: 25,729   Ref: P Jones
West Ham United (2) 2 Kitson 26 Berkovic 44
Blackburn Rovers (2) 1 Gallacher 3 Sutton 62

It was an eventful first half. Kevin Gallacher gave Rovers the lead after just three minutes. Then the Scottish striker was dismissed for elbowing Eyal Berkovic who put West Ham ahead on the stroke of half-time.

103 minutes:
John Hartson guides the ball past stand-in Rovers keeper Fettis to give West Ham the lead

114 minutes:
A rare header from Stuart Ripley brings Rovers level

Penalty shoot-out:
Colin Hendry misses first spot-kick of the night and Lomas converts to send West Ham through

John Hartson put West Ham ahead in extra-time, but Rovers' Ripley equalised

5TH ROUND (REPLAY)

Wolverhampton 2   Wimbledon 1

Robinson 63, Freedman 85

Jones 48

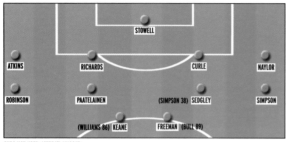

SUBS NOT USED: MURRAY, MUSCAT

SUBS NOT USED: HEALD, REEVES

With chairman Sir Jack Hayward tiring of being used as a 'Golden Tit', Mark McGhee had to tighten the Wolves purse strings. But the Wolves overcame the Wombles...

Att: 25,122 Ref: U D Rennie

Wolves booked their passage to the Quarter-finals for the third time in eight years thanks to a late goal from Dougie Freedman. Mark McGhee's men overcame Wimbledon at the second attempt after earning a 1-1 draw at Selhurst Park. In the first game, Mixu Paatelainen's equaliser after the interval cancelled out an early Jason Euell strike and Wolves, backed by 10,000 travelling supporters, spent much of the second half on the offensive. Despite their ascendancy, Wolves skipper Keith Curle was happy to take the Dons back to Molineux: "It will be different in the replay and we're not going to say anything to wind them

up. Wimbledon haven't changed at all since I was here – I've still got the lumps to prove it," he said.

Wimbledon captain Vinnie Jones gave the Premiership side a second half lead in the replay. But Wolves, backed by 25,000 fans and inspired by the youthful exuberance of 17-year old Robbie Keane, drew level just after the hour when Carl Robinson nodded home from Mark Atkins' deep cross. Both teams had their chances in the ensuing exchanges, but in the final minutes, former Palace striker Dougie Freedman nudged the ball past Chris Perry and struck a

Did you know?
When Wimbledon beat Liverpool 1-0 at Wembley, John Aldridge became the first player to miss a penalty in an FA Cup Final

fantastic 30 yard drive into the top corner. "If we had got a second goal we would have won comfortably," said Dons boss Joe Kinnear, afterwards. And he added: "It was a case of we missed our chances and they took theirs, but for Gayle to fail to hit the target from the six-yard line when no-one is near him is not really on."

Wolves manager Mark McGhee was ecstatic at a result which paved their way to a Quarter-final tie against Leeds. "It was difficult at times to deal with Wimbledon's crosses, but I always felt we could do it and Freedman's goal was sensational," he said.

FIRST MATCH	REPLAY

FIRST MATCH
Saturday 14 February   Att: 15,322   Ref: U D Rennie
Wimbledon (1) 1 Euell
Wolverhampton Wanders (0) 1 Paatelainen
Mixu Paatelainen rescued Wolves with a second half equaliser, after Jason Euell had given the Dons the lead before the break. Backed by 10,000 fans, Wanderers rallied to take the tie back to Molineux

REPLAY

48 minutes:
Vinnie Jones heads home Neil Ardley's third successive corner

63 minutes:
Wolves level when Carl Robinson nods Atkins' cross past Sullivan

85 minutes:
Dougie Freedman picks up a clearance from Stowell, rounds Chris Perry and shoots a 30 yard winner

Carl Robinson celebrates scoring
Wanderers' vital equalising goal

Quiz Four

Test your football knowledge

1 Crystal Palace beat Liverpool 4-3 in the 1990 Semi-final at Villa Park. But by what score did they lose at Anfield in the league earlier that season?
a) 7-0   b) 8-0   c) 9-0

2 Which team has made the most appearances in FA Cup Semi-finals?
a) Manchester United   b) Everton   c) Liverpool

3 In which year did Wembley first stage an FA Cup Semi-final?
a) 1991   b) 1992   c) 1993

4 Who scored the winner for Everton in the 1995 Final against Manchester United?
a) Duncan Ferguson   b) Graham Stuart   c) Paul Rideout

5 Paul Gascoigne was stretchered off in the 1991 Final against Nottingham Forest after a rash challenge. Who did he tackle?
a) Des Walker   b) Gary Charles   c) Gary Parker

6 When Coventry beat Tottenham in the 1987 FA Cup Final, who scored a goal after just 120 seconds?
a) Keith Houchen   b) Clive Allen   c) Dave Bennett

7 Tommy Hutchinson scored for both Manchester City and Spurs in the 1981 Final. Who struck twice in the replay?
a) Ossie Ardiles   b) Ricardo Villa   c) Steve Archibald

8 Chesterfield lost to Middlesbrough in the 1997 Semi-final. But at which ground?
a) Hillsborough   b) Old Trafford   c) Villa Park

9 When Everton won the cup in 1995, which team did they beat 4-1 in the Semi-final at Elland Road?
a) Crystal Palace   b) Chelsea   c) Tottenham

10 Which league club has won the most FA Cup ties in the last 10 years?
a) Arsenal   b) Manchester United   c) Liverpool

Sean Dyche played in a Semi-final for Chesterfield, but where? (Question 8)

THE ANSWERS

1c 2b 3a 4c 5b 6b 7b 8a 9b 10b

THE QUARTER-FINALS OF THE FA CUP

Down to the last eight, and just two games away from the Final, the Wembley showpiece beckons. George Graham must have been confident when Leeds landed their fourth home tie against lower league opposition in a row, but Wolverhampton Wanderers emerged victorious. Arsenal needed a replay to overcome Crystal Palace, and Sheffield United's Alan Kelly made three amazing penalty saves...

QUARTER-FINALS

Arsenal 1   West Ham United 1

Bergkamp 26 (pen)   Pearce 12

SUBS NOT USED: GARDE, UPSON, LUKIC, HUGHES

SUBS NOT USED: FORREST, BISHOP, MEAN, HODGES

Arsenal finally overcame a battling West Ham United after a replay and a tense penalty shoot-out at Upton Park. Stand-in keeper Alex Manninger was the Gunners' hero, making crucial blocks to deny the Hammers in extra-time, before saving Eyal Berkovic's spot kick... Att: 38,077 Ref: M D Reed

This Quarter-final tie at Highbury ended in a free-for-all when Patrick Vieira lashed out at John Moncur and then Frank Lampard. Vieira reacted angrily after Hammers midfielder Moncur collided with him seconds before the end of the match, and it led to players from both sides wading in. Fortunately, no damage was done, but the referee's whistle signified an excellent draw for West Ham, who defended stoutly against a strong Arsenal side. The Gunners could have taken the lead as early as the first minute when Ray Parlour's forceful run was brought to an abrupt halt by Steve Potts. Dennis Bergkamp engineered an excellent free-kick over the wall but Bernard Lama tipped it over the bar. West Ham took a shock lead on 12 minutes, when Ian Pearce fired home from Frank Lampard's low corner. Arsenal levelled before the break when Dennis Bergkamp converted a penalty, after Pearce had up-ended Martin Keown in the box. The Gunners' rookie Austrian keeper Alex Manninger made a couple of good saves to deny West Ham either side of the interval, but Arsenal always looked the more likely. Their best second half chance came when Marc Overmars centred, but Lama saved acrobatically with substitute Christopher Wreh waiting to pounce. The result disappointed Arsène Wenger. "We should have won but we didn't get enough players into the opposition box," he said.

Hammers' boss Harry Redknapp thought his team had worked hard to earn a replay. "We certainly deserved to draw considering the side I had to put out. Rio Ferdinand, Steve Lomas and Ian Pearce were all carrying injuries." And so to Upton Park and the replay...

Did you know? Former Hammers skipper Bobby Moore was a losing finalist AGAINST West Ham when he was in the Fulham side that lost 2-0

KEY MOMENTS: FIRST GAME AT HIGHBURY

1 minute: Dennis Bergkamp strikes a superb free-kick after Parlour is hauled down, but Lama makes a flying save

12 minutes: Ian Pearce fires home from close range for West Ham after Rio Ferdinand dummies Lampard's low struck corner-kick

26 minutes: Pearce goes from hero to villain when he pulls down Keown in 18 yard area. Bergkamp converts the spot-kick

38 minutes: Already-booked West Ham skipper Lomas deliberately handles the ball. Referee lets him off with a warning

74 minutes: Arsenal sub Christopher Wreh is denied by Lama's acrobatics

90 minutes: Vieira lashes out at Moncur sparking a free-for-all. Vieira goes unpunished

England defenders Rio Ferdinand and
Martin Keown battle for the ball

QUARTER-FINALS (REPLAY)

West Ham United 1   Arsenal 1

Hartson 84   *Anelka 45*

SUBS NOT USED: FORREST, BISHOP, MEAN, HODGES

SUBS NOT USED: LUKIC, GRIMANDI

Att: 25,859   Ref: M D Reed

Arsenal booked their place in the Semi-final at Upton Park after a tense penalty shoot-out. John Hartson and Samassi Abou both hit the same post and Berkovic saw his spot-kick saved by Alex Manninger. Dennis Bergkamp was left to contemplate his actions after he was sent off for violent conduct in the first half, when he lashed out at Steve Lomas. "It was stupid, it was just a reaction after he had pulled at my shirt and I didn't realise the consequences because it happened in a split-second," said the striker afterwards. "The team suffer and so do I – they know how I feel and now I'm looking from the outside when the Semi-final is played. I'm sure they can make Wembley without me because they have such magnificent spirit."

That Arsenal survived without Bergkamp is testament to the team spirit he referred to. The Gunners took an unexpected lead just before half-time, when Anelka latched onto an excellent pass from Vieira to shoot past Lama. West Ham fought tooth and nail for an equaliser and were rewarded six minutes from the end when their top scorer John Hartson struck a near-post shot past Manninger. Although the Hammers had the better of the chances in extra-time, Arsenal held on and won the shoot-out. "We needed a miracle when West Ham equalised," said Arsène Wenger. "I couldn't see how we were going to score, we just needed luck on our side. Once the game went into extra-time

and we had to make so many substitutions, the only way we were going to score was from the penalty spot. We showed typical Arsenal spirit and mental toughness. I don't think many teams could have resisted like that." For Harry Redknapp, his side was left with one less route to European competition next season. "I couldn't have asked any more of my players. It would have been nice to go to the Semi-final. I felt we deserved that after the way we've played this season," said the Hammers' boss.

Did you know?
Including 1998, Arsenal have appeared in 13 FA Cup finals. Only Manchester United can better this record – they've been in 14

MAN OF THE MATCH: ALEX MANNINGER
The young Austrian goalkeeper, who kept six consecutive Premiership clean sheets when David Seaman was sidelined, was in outstanding form yet again. Manninger, more than any other Arsenal player denied West Ham victory in the replay. He kept out John Hartson and Lee Hodges in normal time, and made saves from John Moncur and Frank Lampard in extra-time. Then he saved Eyal Berkovic's spot-kick.

KEY MOMENTS: REPLAYED GAME AT UPTON PARK   Arsenal win 4-3 on penalties after extra time

34 minutes:
Dennis Bergkamp is dismissed for lashing out at Steve Lomas, leaving the West Ham skipper's nose bloodied

37 minutes:
Lomas returns to the fray. Bergkamp does not

45 minutes:
10-man Arsenal take the lead when Nicholas Anelka slides home after neat work from Patrick Vieira

84 minutes:
Hammers equalise when John Hartson turns neatly and fires past Manninger at the near post

120 minutes:
Manninger saves Berkovic's spot kick. Hartson and Abou strike the post, and Arsenal progress to the Semi-finals

A jubilant Arsenal congratulate their young
Austrian goalkeeper, Alex Manninger

QUARTER-FINALS

Coventry City 1   Sheffield United 1

Dublin 32 (pen)

Marcelo 45

SUBS NOT USED: SHAW, HAWORTH, HOWIE

SUBS NOT USED: DELLOS, LUDLAM, TRACEY

Sheffield United booked their place in the last four after a dramatic penalty shoot-out, in which keeper Alan Kelly emerged as a hero. Kelly saved three consecutive spot kicks to break the hearts of Coventry and earned the Blades a Semi-final tie against Newcastle... Att: 23,084 Ref: S W Dunn

After one of the most turbulent weeks in their history, Sheffield United were delighted to come away from Highfield Road with a draw. Earlier in the week, Bramall Lane had been in turmoil following the resignations of manager Nigel Spackman and chairman Mike McDonald. Ex-Blades centre-half Steve Thompson took over and was delighted with his appointment. "I'm Sheffield United through and through, I supported them as a kid, I played for them and now I want to continue helping them as a coach," he said.

But the draw was a big disappointment for Coventry, who had come into the game on the back of six successive victories. The Premiership side could have gone ahead early in the game when Darren Huckerby cut in from the left, but his shot was saved at the near post by Alan Kelly. Then Noel Whelan squandered a good chance when he blasted over from close range, after Kelly had saved his initial header. However, City took the lead just after the half hour mark when Nicky Marker's trailing leg up-ended Gavin Strachan in the box. Dion Dublin, playing at centre-half, converted the penalty-kick, which was at least what Coventry deserved at this stage of the game. But just as Strachan's men thought they would take that one goal lead into the interval, United struck back. The hitherto anonymous Brazilian striker Marcelo danced past Dublin and swept a glorious drive in off the post.

The referee was checking his watch when Steve Ogrizovic raced 20 yards from his goal to make a clearance. But the ball struck Petr Katchouro who returned it goal-ward, only for Ogrizovic to make a dramatic recovery, much to Coventry's relief.

Did you know?
Coventry City's only FA Cup win was against Spurs in 1987. Tottenham have appeared in the final nine times

KEY MOMENTS: FIRST GAME AT HIGHFIELD ROAD

29 minutes:
Noel Whelan's header is saved by Kelly, but Whelan misses the rebound from just yards out

32 minutes:
Nicky Marker brings down Gavin Strachan in the box and Dion Dublin converts to give Coventry the lead

45 minutes:
Brazilian striker Marcelo skips past Dublin and fires home the equaliser

88 minutes:
Ogrizovic is nearly embarrassed when his clearance hits Petr Katchouro. Oggie is relieved to see the ball bounce past the post

Dion Dublin shows the skill which made
him joint top-scorer in the Premiership

QUARTER-FINALS (REPLAY)

Sheffield United 1   Coventry City 1

Holdsworth 89   Telfer 10

SUBS NOT USED: BEARD, TRACEY

SUBS NOT USED: HOWIE, WILLIAMS, SHILTON

Att: 29,034 Ref: S W Dunn

Alan Kelly was the toast of Bramall Lane after he pulled off three spectacular penalty saves to break Coventry hearts in a dramatic shoot-out. The Republic of Ireland international denied Dion Dublin, David Burrows and Simon Haworth. Only Paul Telfer managed to convert a spot-kick for Coventry. Roger Nilsen, Bobby Ford and Wayne Quinn tucked their penalties away safely to book United's place in the last four. It was double delight for Kelly, for he was the only survivor from the Blades' side that reached the Semi-finals in 1993. Gordon Strachan must have been dreaming of a Semi-final meeting with Newcastle United when his side led the tie with just a minute remaining on the clock. But in the 89th minute, Coventry failed to clear a

corner and Roger Nilsen's nod-down was met by a stinging half-volley from skipper David Holdsworth, probably the Blades' best player on the night. It was justice for a Sheffield United side that had looked the more likely to score, particularly after the first half hour. Coventry took an early lead in the 10th minute when Paul Telfer slid the ball past Alan Kelly, but despite recent good form, the Sky Blues couldn't capitalise on their lead. Strachan's men passed the ball neatly for 30 minutes and rarely gave United any opportunity to register in the final third. In the second half, the home side stepped up a gear. Petr Katchouro replaced Craig Short in the 64th minute as United pushed men forward. At the

Did you know?
When United met neighbours Wednesday in the 1993 Semi-final, the teams played at Wembley in order to satisfy ticket demand

other end, Coventry striker Viorel Moldovan missed a glorious opportunity to wrap the game up before Holdsworth's last gasp strike. United could have snatched victory in extra-time but Coventry held on for a penalty shoot-out.

Gareth Taylor's penalty strike was easily saved by Coventry veteran Steve Ogrizovic. But then Alan Kelly took centre stage and Sheffield United marched on. Kelly admitted afterwards that he'd only ever saved one penalty in his life before that shoot-out.

MAN OF THE MATCH ALAN KELLY
There was only one choice for Man of the match after the Blades won the penalty shoot-out, thanks to their Republic of Ireland international keeper Kelly. He produced three sensational saves to deny Dion Dublin, Simon Haworth and David Burrows. And it was Kelly who saved United in the first game at Highfield Road with some great stops.

KEY MOMENTS: REPLAYED GAME AT BRAMALL LANE   Sheffield United win 3-1 on penalties aet

10 minutes:
Paul Telfer opens Coventry's account as the Sky Blues dominate the early exchanges in the game

89 minutes:
Blades' skipper David Holdsworth volleys in from 12 yards to take the match into extra-time

120 minutes:
Ogrizovic saves Gareth Taylor's weak spot-kick

120 minutes:
Kelly rattles off three consecutive penalty saves

120 minutes:
Wayne Quinn converts to send United into the Quarter-finals

QUARTER-FINALS

Leeds United 0   Wolverhampton 1

Don Goodman 82

SUB NOT USED: WETHERALL, HOPKIN, BOWYER, BEENEY

SUBS NOT USED: STOWELL, SIMPSON, ATKINS, ROBERTS

Leeds were on an excellent run of form in the league when Wolves arrived at Elland Road. United were expected by most pundits to win the tie at a canter, but they hadn't banked on Wolves playing with three strikers. Mark McGhee's tactics were spot on...

Att: 39,902 Ref: P Durkin,

Wolverhampton Wanderers progressed to the Semi-finals with a dramatic win over Leeds United at Elland Road. Although George Graham's men had most of the possession, Don Goodman sealed a win for the Nationwide League side when he latched onto Carl Robinson's through-ball and neatly clipped the ball over Nigel Martyn in the 82nd minute. Yet just six minutes later, Leeds could easily have rescued the tie when Jimmy Floyd Hasselbaink was judged to have been fouled in the box by Wolves' substitute Robbie Keane. Hasselbaink, the £2m close season signing from Boavista, stepped up to

take the kick but Hans Segers dived to his left and made an easy save. "I was able to make that stop from Jimmy because I do my homework," said a jubilant Segers afterwards. "I have watched him take penalties on Match of the Day before and noticed that he always puts them to the keeper's left." After the kick Keith Curle made some remarks to Hasselbaink who reacted angrily, appearing to headbutt the Wolves skipper, but Don Goodman stepped in to calm the situation down. "Jimmy only did what he did out of

Did you know?
Leeds United manager George Graham played for Arsenal in the 1971 FA Cup Final when they beat Liverpool 2-1 to complete the domestic double

frustration," said Curle. "There is no harm done as far as I am concerned."

Leeds should have opened their account as early as the fifth minute when Rod Wallace scampered onto a pass from Alf-Inge Haaland. Although Wallace outpaced the Wolves' defence, he skewed his shot wide when Harry Kewell, who was in close attendance, was better placed for a strike on goal. And young Australian wide-man Kewell should have scored just before the half hour mark, when he latched onto the ball after a slip from Carl Robinson, but the youngster struck his

KEY MOMENTS: FIRST HALF

5 minutes:
Rod Wallace latches onto a through ball from Alf-Inge Haaland but screws his shot wide

7 minutes:
Wolves retaliate but Dougie Freedman's shot just clears the bar after a nod-down from Bull

28 minutes:
Harry Kewell scampers down the left, but with only Segers to beat he hits the ball straight at the keeper

33 minutes:
Leeds claim a penalty after Wallace tumbles in the area. Paul Durkin waves away the protests

Leeds United 0   Wolverhampton 1

shot straight at Segers from point blank range.

Not that the Leeds' defence was untroubled. Dougie Freedman fashioned a drive which just cleared the bar, and later on, he should have found an unmarked Steve Bull in the box, but his pass went astray.

Leeds turned on the heat after the interval. Jimmy Hasselbaink found Rod Wallace in space, but he delayed his shot and Segers dived bravely at his feet. Then Robert Molenaar headed Gary Kelly's free-kick just over the bar. Haaland missed Leeds' best chance in open play, but he completely miskicked Hasselbaink's nod-down from close range.

Then Wolves silenced the majority of the 40,000 crowd with a superbly worked breakaway goal, finished by Goodman. The Leeds-born striker was delighted with a goal against his hometown team, who rejected him when he was a youngster, apparently because he was too small. "I had 18 months being a ball boy at Elland Road and I had a dream of playing for the club and emulating my all-time hero Peter Lorimer," said Goodman. "I was shattered when they rejected me as a teenager and now, at my age, I have to accept that I will never get the chance to play for Leeds." And Goodman added: "Down the years I always clung to the hope that I would get a crack at playing for United. When I was at West Brom and then Sunderland, I was told that Leeds were watching me and were considering putting in a bid. Nothing ever came of the transfer talk so I just got on with my job doing the best for the club I was playing for."

The defeat was a bitter disappointment for Leeds' boss George Graham, in his first full season in charge. "We probably had too many players in the team today not playing anywhere near their capabilities. We had a great opportunity to get into the last four but we weren't up to it," he said. And he added: "I didn't think we deserved to win the game but I didn't think we

Did you know?
Wolves beat Blackburn 3-0 in the 1960 final. Rovers' Dave Whelan was carried off with a broken leg. He is now owner of JJB Sports and Wigan chairman

deserved to lose it. They worked hard in midfield and they kept us stretched at the back without making many chances. Nigel Martyn's not really made a save. Having said that, we were fortunate to get a penalty in the last couple of minutes, we had an opportunity but never took it. That just sums up the game for us. Probably, looking back on it, I should just have said, 'We're only playing with half a team today so we've just got to settle for a draw and go away and probably win it away'." The defeat left Graham's side to concentrate their efforts in qualifying for a UEFA Cup spot, which they comfortably managed in the end.

For Mark McGhee's men, the win kept Wolves season alive, after their disappointing league form meant they missed out on the play-offs yet again, with speculation rife that McGhee's position as boss was in doubt.

"I have to accept that I will never get the chance to play for Leeds"
Wolves' striker Don Goodman, a lifelong Leeds United fan

"We probably had too many players in the team today not playing anywhere near their capabilities"
George Graham points the finger of blame at his players

MAN OF THE MATCH: HANS SEGERS
The Wolves keeper kept Leeds' in-form frontmen at bay all afternoon, making numerous saves from Jimmy Floyd Hasselbaink, Rodney Wallace and Harry Kewell. Segers' performance was made all the sweeter by the fact he had only recently escaped the threat of a jail sentence. He was accused of match-fixing in a high-profile court case. Segers was only playing because Wolves' regular keeper Mike Stowell was injured.

KEY MOMENTS: SECOND HALF

47 minutes:
Segers again denies Leeds, diving at the feet of Hasselbaink

79 minutes:
Haaland misses an easy chance, fluffing his shot when laid on by Hasselbaink

82 minutes:
Wolves break the deadlock when Goodman latches onto a through ball from Robinson and clips it over Martyn

88 minutes:
Robbie Keane brings down Hasselbaink in the box, but the Dutch striker's penalty is second-guessed by Hans Segers who makes a great save

Harry Kewell, Leeds' exciting Australian winger, will have to wait for Cup glory

QUARTER-FINALS

Newcastle United 3

Ketsbaia 16, Speed 26, Batty 90

Barnsley 1

Liddell 56

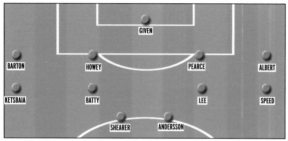

SUBS NOT USED: HISLOP, PEACOCK, BARNES, TOMASSON, HAMILTON

SUBS: LEESE, JONES, TINKLER

Newcastle's Northern Ireland winger Keith Gillespie missed the match against Barnsley after an affray with team-mates outside a Dublin pub. To the football world, it seemed that Dalglish's side was in turmoil, but they raised their game against the Tykes...

Att: 36,695 Ref: P Jones,

Newcastle United put their abysmal Premiership form to one side when they beat a battling Barnsley side 3-1, in a match which was a tremendous advertisement for FA Cup football. With the Premiership taking precedent for many clubs, it had been suggested in some quarters that the world's most famous domestic trophy didn't have the same glamour as it used to. Try telling that to the Toon Army at the end of this match. The result was important to the morale of Dalglish's side, in another week when Newcastle hit the headlines for all the wrong reasons. A short break in Dublin left Northern Ireland winger

Keith Gillespie nursing a broken cheekbone after an alleged fracas with Alan Shearer outside a bar. Gillespie was considered unfit to take any part in the game, but his enforced absence enabled Georgian international midfielder Temuri Ketsbaia to start for the first time in three months.

It was Ketsbaia who almost fashioned a lead on four minutes. Newcastle won a free-kick on the edge of the box, but the Georgian's dead-ball strike clipped the outside of the upright. However, 12 minutes later, United took the lead.

Did you know?
Newcastle's all-time top scorer is Jackie Milburn, who once scored after just 45 seconds in an FA Cup Final

Gary Speed, still trying to win over the Toon Army, swept the ball to Robert Lee and he neatly laid the ball into the path of Ketsbaia who powered into the box before driving a low shot under the body of David Watson. TV replays later suggested that Ketsbaia might have been in an offside position, but the goal stood.

Newcastle doubled their lead 10 minutes later. Robert Lee was again instrumental in its creation, sliding an intelligent ball through to Andreas Andersson and, although Watson did well to block the Swedish striker's shot, the ball rebounded to

KEY MOMENTS: FIRST HALF

4 minutes:
Temuri Ketsbaia hits a tremendous free-kick but it clips the outside of the post

16 minutes:
Ketsbaia latches onto the ball after good work from Gary Speed and Rob Lee to fire home from 12 yards

26 minutes:
Lee sends in Andreas Andersson. His shot is saved by Watson but Speed fires home the rebound

33 minutes:
Neil Redfearn serves notice that Barnsley are not finished when his 30 yard strike whistles just wide of an upright

Veteran full-back Stuart Pearce beats
Barnsley striker Ashley Ward to the ball

Newcastle United 3   Barnsley 1

Gary Speed, who finished neatly with a low drive into the bottom corner. It was the Welsh international's first goal since his £5.5m transfer from Everton this season, where he was team captain.

Despite the two goal deficit, Barnsley matched Newcastle throughout the first half and were a considerably different proposition to the side that shipped so many goals in the first half of the season. Indeed, Barnsley were playing the more composed football for much of the first half. The Tykes wasted a couple of chances when Ashley Ward's shot flew across the face of the goal and soon after, Andy Liddell should have made more of an excellent through ball from wing-back Nicky Eaden. Then skipper Neil Redfearn posted notice of Barnsley's intent when he hit an angled 30 yard drive which just whistled past the post.

With Newcastle two goals to the good, Danny Wilson knew that changes had to be made. Centre-half Adrian De Zeeuw was sacrificed and

Barnsley's record signing, Macedonian striker Georgi Hristov entered the fray.

It was just reward for Barnsley when they halved the deficit 12 minutes after the interval. Martin Bullock, who minutes earlier had come on as a substitute, made space on the right and his centre was met by Andy Liddell, who lifted the ball over Shay Given from 12 yards. The goal raised the hopes of Barnsley's 5,000 travelling fans and the Tykes side pressed for an equaliser. But the match turned sour in the space of 16 second half minutes, in which Adrian Moses was sent off for two yellow card offences against Alan Shearer. Barnsley were outraged, claiming that the England skipper made a meal of the challenges.

Shearer almost took advantage of the 10 men, but Watson was equal to his strike, so it was left to a rare goal from David Batty to make the game safe in the final minute. The Yorkshireman struck a low, left foot drive from the edge of the box to send the Geordies

Did you know?
Viv Anderson became the first black manager in the history of English football when Barnsley appointed him in 1993

into an Old Trafford showdown with Sheffield United. Newcastle manager Kenny Dalglish was annoyed at the number of cards the referee flourished throughout the game: "The match didn't merit 10 bookings, because there were no nasty tackles. Both sets of players played in the right spirit, and it was tremendous entertainment for the fans. I thought it was a tremendous match. The boys have been getting a bit of stick all week, but this win was due to the calibre of person that they are." Dalglish also had a word for Danny Wilson's spirited team: "Barnsley never gave up, but they had a mountain to climb because we started so well. They hung in there and did everything they possibly could, but in the end we deserved to win."

Kenny Dalglish's first full season in charge has hardly been an unqualified success, but the win gave Newcastle a chance to save their season.

> "The boys have been getting a bit of stick all week, but this win was due to the calibre of person that they are"
> Kenny Dalglish praises his players after the match

> "Barnsley never gave up, but they had a mountain to climb because we started so well"
> And Kenny has a magnanimous word for his defeated opponents too

MAN OF THE MATCH ROB LEE
With Alan Shearer failing to register, all Newcastle's goals came from an energetic midfield, superbly marshalled by skipper Robert Lee. The England international set up all three for his team-mates and kept his defensive discipline at the other end.

KEY MOMENTS: SECOND HALF

57 minutes:
Martin Bullock, a recent substitute crosses for Andy Liddell who fires past Shay Given from 12 yards

67 minutes:
Barnsley waste a glorious opportunity to equalise when shots from Ashley Ward and Darren Sheridan are blocked on the line

69 minutes:
David Watson pulls off a superb save from Shearer's header after a neat chip from Steve Howey

74 minutes:
Adrian Moses receives his second yellow card for a foul on Shearer and is dismissed from the field of play

90 minutes:
A rare goal from David Batty settles the match. The Yorkshireman's left-foot drive from outside the box finds the bottom corner

Newcastle's Republic of Ireland keeper
Shay Given celebrates the victory

Quiz Five

Test your football knowledge

1 Tottenham were taken to a replay in the 1982 Final by QPR. Who scored for Spurs in both ties?

a) Hoddle   b) Archibald   c) Crooks

2 When Manchester United met Crystal Palace in the 1990 Final, Ian Wright came off the bench to bag a brace at Wembley. Who scored twice for United?

a) Robson   b) Hughes   c) Martin

3 Which of these Premiership clubs has never won the FA Cup?

a) Leicester City   b) Blackburn Rovers   c) Derby County

4 Who is the only player to have been sent off in an FA Cup Final?

a) Peter Reid   b) Ron 'Chopper' Harris   c) Kevin Moran

5 Who was the Smith immortalised in the fanzine title, 'And Smith Must Score' when he missed a sitter for Brighton against Manchester United in 1983?

a) Dennis Smith   b) Tommy Smith   c) Gordon Smith

6 Who is the youngest player to appear in an FA Cup Final?

a) Paul Allen   b) Norman Whiteside   c) Howard Kendall

7 Who was the last team to reach the FA Cup Final from outside the Premiership?

a) Sunderland   b) Middlesbrough   c) Crystal Palace

8 Who was the manager of Wimbledon when they won the trophy in 1988?

a) Dave Bassett   b) Bobby Gould   c) Joe Kinnear

9 When was the first FA Cup Final played at Wembley Stadium?

a) 1926   b) 1920   c) 1923

10 When was the last 100,000 crowd for an FA Cup Final?

a) 1984   b) 1985   c) 1986

Tottenham pose for pictures after their 1982 FA Cup victory. (Question 1)

THE ANSWERS

1a 2b 3a 4c 5c 6a 7a 8b 9c 10 b

THE SEMI-FINALS OF THE FA CUP

It's often said that it's worse to lose in the Semi-final of the cup than it is the Final. No-one remembers the teams who are dispatched at this stage, and the fans don't get their day out at Wembley. This year, the Uniteds of Newcastle and Sheffield met at Old Trafford, while Wolverhampton Wanderers made the short trip to Villa Park where they met an in-form Arsenal chasing the domestic double...

SEMI-FINALS

Newcastle United 1   Sheffield United 0

Shearer 60

SUBS NOT USED: HISLOP, RUSH, TOMASSON, HUGHES

SUBS NOT USED: SHORT, TRACEY

Newcastle last reached the FA Cup Final in 1974, where they were convincingly beaten by a Liverpool side containing Kevin Keegan. Sheffield United haven't played in the final since 1936, when they lost 1-0 to Arsenal. But in the Semi-final, it was Dalglish's men who prevailed... Att: 53,452 Ref: G Poll

After a season of turmoil, Newcastle United reached the FA Cup Final for the first time in 24 years, after a hard-earned 1-0 victory against Sheffield United. Alan Shearer struck the winner from close range, after Alan Kelly had palmed out his initial header from a John Barnes' centre. It was the England skipper's fifth goal of Newcastle's cup campaign and the third time he had scored the winning goal.

The Magpies had suffered a dreadful Premiership campaign in Kenny Dalglish's first full season in charge, and aside from a memorable 3-2 Champions' League victory over Barcelona, the Geordie faithful had little to shout about. With Dalglish foregoing the cavalier nature of Keegan's team, but retaining his dour public image, Newcastle lost a lot of goodwill around the country. Their cause wasn't helped after the unseemly public wrangle with Stevenage Borough regarding the Conference side's right to stage the tie at Broadhall Way. Then Keith Gillespie was left sprawled on a pavement outside a Dublin bar, after an alleged bust-up with Alan Shearer. The Northern Ireland winger, nursing a

Did you know?
Sheffield United won the 1915 FA Cup final, known as the 'Khaki Final' because the of the number of spectators in army uniform

fractured cheekbone, missed Newcastle's next game. Worse was to come. Remarks made in a Spanish brothel by United directors Douglas Hall and Freddie Shepherd hit newspaper headlines and the two were forced to resign after an outcry by the fans.

Sheffield United were in similar straits, following the departure of manager Nigel Spackman and chairman Mike McDonald. Former United defender Steve Thompson took the reigns for the Blades' first Semi-final appearance since their defeat by neighbours Wednesday in 1993.

KEY MOMENTS: FIRST HALF

5 minutes:
Bobby Ford gets in the first shot of the game but it isn't strong enough to trouble Shay Given

8 minutes:
Gary Speed heads onto the roof of the net from a well-placed Dabizas cross

18 minutes:
Alan Shearer releases Andreas Andersson. But the Swede lets the ball run too far and his weak shot is cleared by Sandford

22 minutes:
Nicos Dabizas slices his attempted clearance into the path of Wayne Quinn who centres, only for Marcelo to loop over a header

31 minutes:
John Barnes releases Andersson with a fine ball, but Andersson can't match it with a quality finish

Newcastle's £5.5m signing Gary Speed
tussles with Blade Vas Borbokis

Newcastle United 1   Sheffield United 0

Gary Speed, the former Everton skipper signed by Dalglish for £5.5million, came closest to breaking the deadlock in the opening exchanges. Greek defender Nicos Dabizas crossed from the right but Speed's header looped over the Sheffield keeper Alan Kelly and landed on the roof of the net. Andreas Andersson, Newcastle's £3.6million striker from AC Milan, without a goal in seven first team outings, could have helped himself to a first half hat-trick. His first chance came when Shearer flicked on a clever pass from David Batty. The Swede collected the ball but Alan Kelly blocked him on the penalty spot. The ball rebounded back off Andersson towards the net but Lee Sandford cleared off the line. Soon after, the former AC Milan man angled a low drive which Kelly blocked, and then, with the goal at his mercy, Andersson instead tried to set up Gillespie.

It was one-way traffic for most of the first period and, although Marcelo almost beat

Did you know?
Frank Watt managed Newcastle United to six FA Cup Finals between 1905 and 1924, still a record for one man to this day

Shay Given with a header, Steve Thompson must have been the more relieved to go in at the break goalless.

Five minutes after the break, Nicky Marker's cross-field ball was collected by Wayne Quinn, who struck a powerful drive which Given did well to fist over the bar. Seconds later Stuart Pearce managed to block a volley from Graham Stuart. But just as the Yorkshiremen seemed to be in the ascendancy, Newcastle broke down the left, and when Shearer's initial header from Barnes' cross was blocked by Kelly, the England captain followed up the rebound to break the deadlock. Sheffield United rallied and after Dabizas had sliced over his own bar, Warren Barton did well to deny Dean Saunders after excellent work from Stuart. The Blades almost snatched a last gasp equaliser when Wayne Quinn powered in a towering header, but Given made a brilliant fingertip save. The Geordies held on to ensure a trip to the Twin Towers on May 16th where they met Arsenal.

> **"A day out at Wembley is not bad compensation for some of the performances we've been putting in recently"**
> Kenny Dalglish reflects on a poor season for Newcastle outside the Cup

> **"I knew it would be difficult. It wasn't our day"**
> Steve Thompson reflects on a costly defeat

Kenny Dalglish dedicated Newcastle's win to the fans: "I'm delighted, we thoroughly deserved to win and everyone made a contribution. The result is the most important since I've been here but I'm more pleased for the supporters than I am for myself," he said. He added: "We have said often enough that they deserve better than we have been serving up in the league. A day out at Wembley is not a bad compensation for some of the performances we've been putting in recently. They must have been disappointed with some of our results so this is a bit of satisfaction they can take from the season."

Blades' boss Steve Thompson was disappointed but remained upbeat: "Newcastle have got quality players and after the first half, when they hit the post and had a couple kicked off the line, I knew it would be difficult. It wasn't our day."

MAN OF THE MATCH: ALAN SHEARER
Once again, the England skipper proved to be Newcastle's talisman. He scored in both ties against Stevenage and struck the winner in the Quarter-final against Tranmere. With the Semi-final in deadlock, it was Shearer who came through yet again. Indeed, had Newcastle's earlier chances fallen to Shearer the victory would probably have been assured earlier.

KEY MOMENTS: SECOND HALF

50 minutes:
Blades midfielder Nicky Marker finds Wayne Quinn who fires in a shot which Shay Given fists over

51 minutes:
A cross from the left deceives Given. Graham Stuart hits a fine volley but Stuart Pearce blocks

59 minutes:
Shearer heads down Barnes' cross. Kelly palms out, but Shearer follows in to crash home the winner

70 minutes:
Shearer works an opening for Andersson, but he's tackled by Sandford. Shearer collects and hits a 25 yard strike which Borbokis clears

92 minutes:
Sheffield United miss a glorious opportunity. A deep cross is met by a flying header from Wayne Quinn, but Given saves the day for Newcastle

Gary Speed comforts his disconsolate
former Everton teammate Graham Stuart

SEMI-FINALS

Arsenal 1   Wolverhampton 0

Wreh 12

SUBS NOT USED: MANNINGER, BOA MORTE

SUBS NOT USED: STOWELL, NAYLOR

Arsenal were in confident mood when they met Wolves at Villa Park. Arsène Wenger had steered his side through choppy Premiership waters earlier in the season, but the Gunners were making a late charge for the league title. What price a domestic double?   Att: 39,372 Ref: S Lodge

Arsenal booked a place in their 13th FA Cup Final with a 1-0 win over Wolverhampton Wanderers at Villa Park. Christopher Wreh struck the only goal of the game in the 12th minute, firing past Hans Segers after excellent work from Man of the match Patrick Vieira. It was the Gunners' fifth 1-0 victory in their previous six games and it kept them on course for a possible domestic double, a feat achieved by Bertie Mee's Arsenal side in 1971.

Arsène Wenger's men always looked the more likely against a Wolves side that couldn't come to terms with the power and pace of Arsenal's French midfield duo, Patrick Vieira and Emmanuel Petit. Wolves, who had successfully stifled Leeds at Elland Road playing three up-front in the previous round, employed the same tactics, but found Arsenal's defensive unit too strong to break down. Front-runners Don Goodman, Steve Claridge and Paul Simpson received little change from the Gunners' back four, despite the absence of Lee Dixon, who was replaced by Gilles Grimandi.

Arsenal, without the suspended Dennis Bergkamp and long-term injury victim Ian Wright, deployed a two-man frontline of Nicolas Anelka and Christopher Wreh. And it was the man signed by Arsene Wenger from Monaco for just £300,000, who ensured Arsenal's progression to Wembley.

Wreh, the cousin of AC Milan striker George Weah, had spent much of the season as a virtual unknown in Wenger's cosmopolitan squad, but in the two games before the semi-final, he scored the winning goals against both Wimbledon and Bolton Wanderers to keep Arsenal's late charge for the Premiership on the rails. "People told me I'd never get a game at Arsenal

Did you know?
Arsenal were the fourth team to complete the domestic double when they won it in 1971. Preston were the first to do it in 1889

KEY MOMENTS: FIRST HALF

12 minutes:
Patrick Vieira powers through the middle, drawing defenders Curle and Richards and sets up Chris Wreh who finishes neatly from inside the area

18 minutes:
Dean Richards' long ball clears Tony Adams. Don Goodman controls it on his chest but David Seaman gathers just in time

22 minutes:
Ray Parlour engineers a 25 yard drive after good work from Anelka but Hans Segers parries

Arsenal's rejuvenated left-back Nigel Winterburn wins the ball for his side

Arsenal 1   Wolverhampton 0

with Wright and Bergkamp, but now I've taken Arsenal to the Cup Final and it's a great feeling," said an elated Wreh afterwards. "I want to play at Wembley because I've never been there and it will be a big occasion."

The goal came when Wanderers' keeper Hans Segers skewed a clearance straight to the feet of Patrick Vieira just inside the Wolves' half. The Frenchman strode majestically towards the opposition penalty area, cleverly drawing the back-pedalling Keith Curle and Dean Richards before rolling a through-ball into the path of the on-rushing Wreh who confidently steered a low drive past Segers.

Arsenal settled and passed the ball crisply for the remainder of the half, but couldn't translate their possession into goals. Emmanuel Petit came close when Steve Froggatt failed to clear but Segers was alert to the danger. Then Marc Overmars was released after neat link play from Wreh and Anelka. Again, Segers held firm. Ray

Parlour's dipping drive tested the keeper before Wolves almost sneaked one in at the other end, Seaman was forced to dash out of his goal to foil Don Goodman.

Two minutes after the interval, Martin Keown was replaced by Steve Bould after a head clash with Steve Sedgley left him dazed, and for the next 20 minutes, Wolves enjoyed their best spell of the game. When Froggatt teased the already-booked Grimandi down the left, his cross was fumbled by David Seaman but Goodman, perhaps surprised by the England keeper's uncharacteristic lapse, blasted over the bar. Goodman was replaced by Black Country stalwart Steve Bull and his introduction almost paid immediate dividends when he poked the ball through to Claridge. Again, Seaman rescued Arsenal, diving at the striker's feet.

With Wolves pushing for an equaliser, the Gunners' might have sealed the game with a couple of breakaway chances.

Did you know?
Under Stan Cullis, Wolves won the First Division in 1958 and 1959, and the FA Cup in 1960, the most successful period in their history

Nigel Winterburn's drive was palmed over and Anelka should have released a well-positioned Petit late on. Wenger's side were well worth their victory.

"We have had an incredible run in the cup – two penalty shoot-outs and three replays," said Arsène Wenger afterwards. "I am very pleased for Chris Wreh. It's interesting that a player who was barely known a couple of months ago has scored the winning goals against Wimbledon, Bolton and now Wolves."

Wanderers' boss Mark McGhee was downcast but conceded that there was a gulf in class between the sides: "We didn't give ourselves much of a chance and we are disappointed for having gifted the game to Arsenal. We get away with mistakes like that in the First Division but, against Arsenal, you need quality to go with your effort."

> **"It's interesting that a player who was barely known a couple of months ago has scored the winning goals against Wimbledon, Bolton and now Wolves"**
>
> Arséne Wenger congratulates himself on his clever buying

> **"We get away with mistakes like that in the First Division"**
>
> Mark McGhee acknowledges the difference in class

MAN OF THE MATCH: PATRICK VIEIRA
The French international midfielder was the dominant force in the game. Wolves had no answer to Vieira's commitment and sure touch on the ball and he set up the goal for Chris Wreh. Wolverhampton Wanderers' boss, Mark McGhee, was very impressed with Vieira. "He's the fittest player I've seen for a while. He reminds me a bit of Graeme Souness at his best. He breaks things down, harrasses people into mistakes and he's always looking for the ball. The tempo he keeps up is unbelievable."

KEY MOMENTS: SECOND HALF

47 minutes:
Arsenal lose the services of Martin Keown due to injury, but have Steve Bould in reserve

52 minutes:
Steve Froggatt's cross deceives Seaman. The keeper drops it but Goodman fires over the bar

60 minutes:
A Paul Simpson strike rebounds off Seaman but Claridge doesn't react with enough speed to punish Arsenal

67 minutes:
Steve Bull enters the fray in place of Goodman and immediately sets up Steve Claridge. Seaman is equal to his strike, and saves

74 minutes:
Marc Overmars releases Nigel Winterburn, but his fierce shot is palmed over by Segers

Ray Parlour is one of the most-improved
midfield players in the Premiership

THE FINAL OF THE FA CUP

And so, the big one. Saturday 16 May 1998, at three o'clock in the afternoon. The venue is Wembley. Arsenal and Newcastle United have made it to the last stage and there's just 90 minutes between one side and glory. For Arsenal it's a chance to win a magnificent "double" Double of Premiership and Cup. For Newcastle United it's about salvaging something from another season that has seen them fail to put any silverware in the St James Park cabinet. Only one team will walk away winners. The players are on the pitch...

Both sets of fans mingle outside the stadium before the kick off and, below, an Ian Wright look-alike mixes it with Newcastle fans

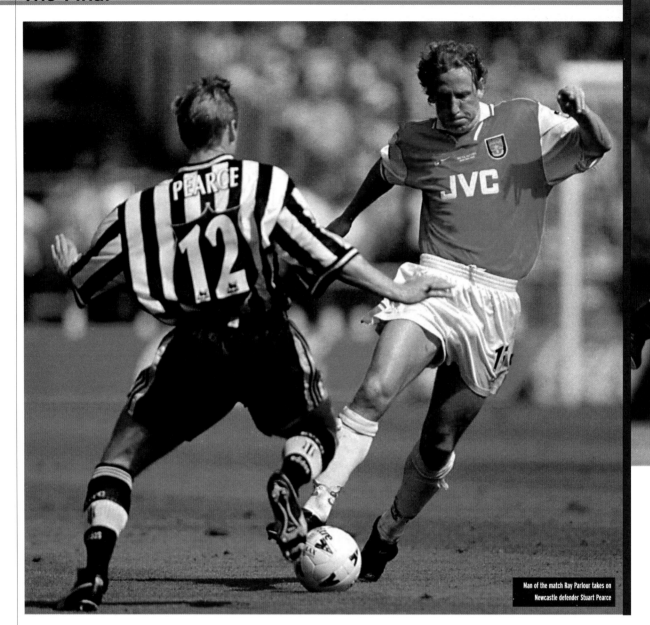

Man of the match Ray Parlour takes on
Newcastle defender Stuart Pearce

T he saddest disappointment of the day must surely be Arsenal star Dennis Bergkamp's relegation to mere spectator. To miss out on the great day seems unfair to the man who has given so much to get the team here.

Equally upset is Ian Wright, who hasn't played 90 minutes since early January, and is passed over for reliable Christopher Wreh. Arsène Wenger is taking no chances.

The match is slow in starting, with both sides taking time to get moving, despite the vocal encouragement from the fans – with the Toon Army in particularly good form.

Finally, after 20 minutes of despondent play, Emmanuel Petit lofts a pass from the half-way line which teammate Overmars chases, closely but unsuccessfully shadowed by Newcastle's Pistone. A left-footed strike from eight yards scores a first goal, and Newcastle must surely scent a whiff of looming

The Dutch winger receives the congratulations
of French teammate Nicolas Anelka

Marc Overmars beats Alessandro Pistone before striking a
low shot under Shay Given for the opening goal – 1–0!

defeat as their desperate attempts to
retaliate disintegrate on Arsenal's rock-
solid defence.

Newcastle's discipline shows signs
of cracking, and Shearer, the lonely
warrior in a team playing it for safety,
gets a booking.

The second half has the Toon Army
roaring their side on to attack, and the
players do their best to respond.

Twice the ball strikes Arsenal's post,
one a header from Dabizas, the second
a Shearer piledriver that beats Seaman
but not the upright.

There will be no more chances for
the men from the North. Sixty-nine
minutes into the game Arsenal score

Arsène Wenger salutes the Gunners' opener. Kenny Dalglish looks grim in the background

again. A pass from Parlour gives Anelka his chance, who leaves Newcastle's Howey standing to angle a scoring shot past goalkeeper Given's right hand.

Newcastle is doomed, despite three chances for Parlour and Speed towards the end.

Arsenal reconfirm that they are Britain's best team this season. Their win against Newcastle has been easy, not even Bergkamp's absence proving a cause for concern. And for Arsène Wenger there's the pride of having led his men to the Double. Time enough for him to prepare for Manchester United's renewed onslaught next season.

Newcastle need to get their act together if they want to achieve a better season next time round. Shearer alone cannot turn a lacklustre side into

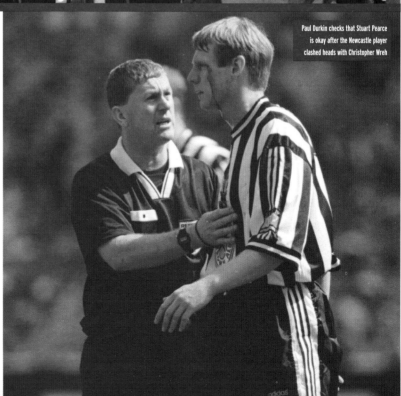

Paul Durkin checks that Stuart Pearce is okay after the Newcastle player clashed heads with Christopher Wreh

Tony Adams gets one-over on his
England colleague Alan Shearer

Alan Shearer is the first player to go into referee Paul Durkin's
book after a reckless challenge on Tony Adams

Arsenal midfielder Patrick Vieira shackles a promising break down the right by Alessandro Pistone

An increasingly frustrated Alan Shearer shouts in the general direction of the referee's assistant

Premiership winners – Dalglish will have his work cut out to rebuild his team's morale.

As for Alan Shearer, he must surely be contemplating the notion that he is wasting his most valuable years on an undeserving side, and that being England captain is not all he should aspire to.

Emmanuel Petit puts in a strong challenge on Gary Speed, who was ineffectual for most of the game

Alan Shearer gets the better of Martin Keown only to see his shot rebound back off the inside of the post

Nicolas Anelka scores Arsenal's second goal, shooting low past Shay Given - 2-0 Arsenal

Arsenal 2   # Newcastle United 0

Overmars 23, Anelka 69   Att: 79,183 Ref: PA Durkin

Arsenal:
SEAMAN
DIXON ADAMS KEOWN WINTERBURN
PARLOUR VIEIRA PETIT OVERMARS
ANELKA WREH (PLATT 62)

Newcastle United:
GIVEN
PISTONE DABIZAS HOWEY PEARCE (ANDERSSON 73)
BARTON (WATSON 76) LEE BATTY SPEED
SHEARER KETSBAIA (BARNES 86)

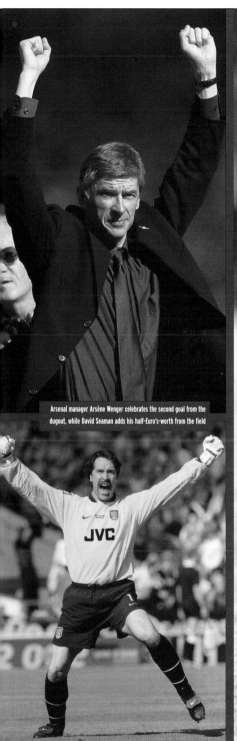

Arsenal manager Arsène Wenger celebrates the second goal from the dugout, while David Seaman adds his half-Euro's-worth from the field

A disconsolate Alan Shearer walks off at the end of the match

Arsenal lift the FA Cup for the seventh time in their history

Arsenal players celebrate their FA Cup win, and the considerable achievement of collecting a domestic Double

F.A. CUP WINNERS 1998

F.A. CUP

SPONSORED BY

LITTLEWOODS

LITTLEWOODS

Men of the match: goalscorers Marc Overmars and Nicolas Anelka parade the FA Cup for Arsenal fans, but don't forget the captain – Tony Adams and Patrick Vieira get their turn...